Journey through the Night

Anne DeVries

Journey through the Night

4. A New Day

PAIDEIA PRESS
St. Catharines, Ontario, Canada

First published in Dutch as *Reis door de nacht*. © G. F. Callenbach BV of Nijkerk. Translated by Harry der Nederlanden.

 Published by Paideia/Premier, P. O. Box 1450, St. Catharines, Ontario, Canada, L2R 7J8.

ISBN 0-88815-754-1
Printed in the United States of America.

A NEW DAY

CHAPTER ONE

When John woke up, he thought he was still in prison, so he kept his eyes closed, trying to recapture his dream. It was a wonderful dream: he was walking across the countryside in his childhood with Father at his side, while in the surrounding fields the farmers were busy bringing in the hay.

But when he stirred, stabbing pains in his knees and arms forced him into consciousness. With a moan he opened his eyes, looking for his cell window. Immediately he sat up in surprise, for above him was a round wooden roof supported by four poles. The bright sunlight and the smell of hay flooded his senses. As he tried to sit up, his hands sank deep into a soft bed of hay. There was hay all around him!

He laughed uncertainly. Now everything was starting to come back to him. He was free! The invasion had begun and soon the war would be over—perhaps. He was on a farm somewhere out in the countryside of

Gelderland, and he had been sleeping. No, not sleeping. He had been unconscious—at least, that was how he felt.

He crawled to the edge of the haystack. Before him lay freedom: a sun-drenched landscape of fields and pastures, the woods hued with a multitude of greens, and nearby a dove was cooing in the branches of a tall pine.

He sank back into the hay, dazzled, and sighed with gratitude. "Lord, please keep me from falling into their hands ever again," he said in his heart. Suddenly he was gripped by the fear that he might not be safe even here. Again he pushed himself up and scanned the countryside in all directions. But there was no hint of danger.

Pale smoke rose peacefully from the chimney of a small white farmhouse nearby, and a woman in an old-fashioned jacket was walking in the yard clucking to the chickens. In the distance, a farmer drove his horse and wagon along a narrow country road. The sun stood high in the sky, presiding over a bright summer day. It was mid-June, John reminded himself, 1944. The last year of the war?

Hadn't the sun been in about the same spot when the farmer brought him here? He must have slept around the clock. No wonder! Once he had realized that the chase was over, he had been so exhausted that he had hardly been able to climb the ladder to the top of the haystack.

Lying back now, he reviewed all that had happened during the past day: mustered into the prison corridor, bounced across the dark countryside in the back of a truck from Amsterdam to Amersfoort and into the sparsely populated countryside of Gelderland, and then the sudden realization that he was being taken into the country to be shot!

A good thing that he had been sitting near the back of the truck! Where had he ever got the courage to jump when the truck was moving that fast? *Had* it been courage on his part? Not really, for it was just as though someone else had done it for him. Then the run through the woods and across the fields, to be found in a small canal, exhausted and bleeding, by a farmer. If the farmer had been a Nazi sympathizer . . . . But he wasn't. He had asked John almost nothing and had taken him straight to his home.

John hadn't been given much time to recover. After washing and while he was still drinking his coffee, the local game warden appeared. The farmer made no attempt to conceal his refugee; apparently the two men were old friends.

"You've got to get him out of here right away!" said the warden excitedly. "You think the Germans are just going to forget about him? As soon as they've got rid of their other prisoners, they'll be back. Either that, or they'll send the police out here!"

The farmer gave John a change of clothes—a pair of overalls and a blue work shirt. But John kept his shoes, which still had the lysol smell of the prison. The warden told him to circle around the farmyard and then head for the woods on the other side of the farm, just in case the Germans came back with tracking dogs.

John cut through the woods, according to instructions, and at the first road the warden met him with an extra bicycle. Then he was led down several back roads for at least an hour before they reached the outlying farm where he was now.

No one had raised a single objection when the warden arrived with his unexpected guest. The old farmer and his wife took John in and cared for him as if it were a matter of course. They fed him until he was full and then fetched a doctor for him, because his arms were badly gouged and one knee was twice its normal size. His abdomen, too, had been severely scraped; apparently he had run full tilt into a barbed-wire fence in the dark. He couldn't remember doing so, but that's what the wound looked like.

After he had been treated, the farmer put him up in the haystack because the house was already full of "divers" hiding from the Nazis. Despite stomach cramps, which he developed because he was no longer used to regular food, he dropped off to sleep almost immediately.

But he was already hungry again this morning. His leg was still stiff, and his joints ached as if they had all been dislocated. But the pain served as a reminder of how fortunate he was.

What was that? A noise close to the haystack! A cough and then the growl of a dog. Suddenly the top of a ladder swung into view, thumping against the haystack, which shook as someone began climbing up. John slid forward on his belly. If it was the enemy, he would kick the ladder over when the man was almost to the top and then try to escape down the other side of the

haystack. But when he peered over the side, he saw the black cap of the farmer bobbing up along the ladder. He lay back and waited until the farmer's leathery face appeared between the top rungs of the ladder. Two slightly mocking eyes met his.

"So there you are!" the man said, grinning. "I thought you were going to sleep all day. But you better pull yourself together and come on down because there's a policeman here for you."

"A policeman!"

"Yeah, but don't worry. He's a friend. He's here to fix you up with an I.D. We're law-abiding citizens hereabouts, you see, and we get our I.D.'s through the police department. I bet you're ready for a bite to eat too, aren't you? How's your knee and your arms? Yeah, you can come down. The coast is clear."

A big German shepherd stood at the foot of the ladder, the hair on his neck bristling. When John got off the ladder, the dog sniffed warily at his pants and shoes.

"It's all right, boy," said the farmer, and then added to John, "Don't pet him. He doesn't like it."

The farmer hid the ladder in the long grass of a nearby ditch and lit his pipe. "Cherry leaves," thought John, coughing from the acrid smoke. He limped a little as they walked to the house, but his leg functioned surprisingly well.

As with most farms in this area, the barn was built adjoining the house, so the farmer cut through the barn on his way to the house. As they entered the barn, a man who had been sweeping the floor quickly slunk into a dark corner. A Jew.

"He's been condemned to death," said the farmer.

"What?"

"This pig. Isn't he a beauty? He'll be the third one this year. We go through quite a bit of meat these days. But I hope he'll be the last one, now that the Allies are finally here. Too bad they're too late to save you, eh, big boy?" He scratched the pig between the ears, and the huge animal grunted happily.

They went into the house and were met at the door by the farmer's wife, who had put on a white bonnet for her company. All the window sills inside the house were filled with flowers. A large, broad figure in uniform rose from the table with extended hand and squeezed John's fingers until his knuckles cracked.

"Congratulations!" boomed the officer. "You were very lucky. Your name is John, right? I'm Van Buren. Tell me, how many of you escaped yesterday?"

"I have no idea. I went on my own, but later I heard shouting, and I remember thinking that some of the others must also have made a run for it."

"At least two more," said Van Buren. "One of them made it. We've got him safely hidden away. The Germans found another man in the woods when they came back with the dogs. He was an old man, and had caught a bullet in the back. But maybe more got away and are wandering around somewhere in the area."

"So they came with tracking dogs, did they?"

"Yes, they were back before ten that morning and picked up your trail right away. They followed your trail to the place of the people who found you, and they were going to search the house there. But that woman sure knows how to handle the Germans. She hollered and scolded. 'You're not coming in here with those dirty boots!' she said. 'I just scrubbed all the floors. Do you think I would let some dirty bum in my clean house? Yes, he came to the door here, but we chased him away. He went that way. I'll show you where he went into the woods.' And they believed her because the dog got no scent of you inside the house. She had used her last bit of soap to scrub down the place.

"So they looked where she pointed and, sure enough, they picked up your trail again. But the dog lost it somewhere in the woods. That was a good idea of the warden to make you go through the woods a ways before giving you a bike. After hunting around for a while, the Germans went back to the point where you had entered the woods. That's when they found the old fellow. Well, now tell me, how do you feel?"

"Great!" said John, swallowing as he thought of the old man who hadn't fared as well as he. His eyes followed the farmer's wife as she sliced a loaf of bread and brought out a plate of pancakes. The coffee smelled delicious.

"You stop talking a minute, Van Buren," she said. "Can't you see the boy's famished? Eat as much as you like, my boy! There's more."

As he ate, John told about the infamous prison in Amsterdam, where he had spent over four months. He also told them about Father, who had been sent to a German concentration camp from the same prison and who might be dead as far as he knew. Mother and his brothers and sisters had taken refuge with a family in

Drenthe. That's where he would like to go too, as quickly as possible.

"So you're from Drenthe, eh? How did you end up in Amsterdam?"

John hesitated. He had learned to tell no more than necessary, even to friends. The policeman noticed his hesitation.

"That's all right," said the man. "All I want to know is, were you in the resistance?"

"Yes. At least . . . ."

"Might I have seen your face in a police bulletin?"

"Over a year ago they printed my picture."

"Then you'll need a good I.D. What kind of work were you involved in? Were you part of a strike squad?"

"Yes."

"Why don't you stay around here? We could use you."

John got a sinking feeling in his stomach that almost took away his appetite. He had barely tasted freedom, and already he was being drawn back into the underground. He really didn't feel ready yet. All he had thought up to now was, "They'll never get their hands on me ever again!"

"I'll tell you what," said Van Buren, "when you're all rested up, we'll talk again. You finished eating? Then, here, have a cigarette."

The farmer had gone back to work, and his wife was busy in the kitchen. Van Buren set John close to a window and opened the curtains wide in order to take his picture without a flash. Then he took out a notebook.

"What should we call you?" he asked John. "Van

Buren, like me? Or Kuiper, Smith, whatever you like."

"De Jong. John De Jong."

"Why that one?"

"It's a common name, which seems a little safer to me."

"Good idea. Occupation? Jobs with the railroad are very popular lately, but you look a little young for that."

"I used to be listed as a school teacher, but I've had enough of teaching. Why don't you just make me a farm hand."

"You don't look like one! Especially not now. Your white jailbird face would give you away."

"Well, then, how about a baker? Or a dairy man? Jobs in the food industry are listed as indispensable, so there's not much chance of being called up to work in Germany."

"Good! We'll make you a baker. We'll also provide you with an exemption from the labor draft. What about your home town? Shall we say you're from Kesteren? The underground destroyed all the town records there, so they can't check you out."

"Then put down Oosterhesselen. Last year the town clerk of Oosterhesselen disappeared with the whole town file."

Van Buren laughed. "Determined to stay in Drenthe, eh? Well, wait a minute, a week or so ago the town hall in Assen was also raided. Don't you think Assen would be better? It would have more bakers than a small town like Oosterhesselen. If you need anything else, let's hear it. I've got to go see the warden and let him know you're not sure whether we should be on the lookout for more escapees."

"I could use another set of clothes," suggested John. "I can't very well go on the train dressed like this."

"True. You don't have much of anything, do you? Don't worry, we'll see that you're fixed up before we let you go."

As Van Buren went out the door, three English fighters screamed by low overhead and disappeared in the distance behind a stand of trees.

"We see them every day now," said the policeman. "They keep strafing the main roads to break down the German supply lines. No trains or automobiles are safe anymore. The other day they even opened up on a baker with a hand cart. The English and the American planes seem to be unchallenged in the air. You hardly ever see a German plane anymore.

"Did you hear the joke about Hitler and Goering getting into a quarrel? They were arguing about how to send the German air force across the channel. Goering wanted to send them in three formations of two, and Hitler in two formations of three. Neat, eh? Well, say goodbye to Mr. Versteeg for me, and try to keep out of sight until we get you your I.D. It should take only a couple days."

But it took considerably longer than two days, and John found the waiting getting harder and harder. There was plenty to keep him busy in the barn and around the yard, however. He ground oats for cereal, cleaned out the pigpen, peeled potatoes for Mrs. Versteeg, and so on. But at the same time his eagerness to see his family, especially Mother and Rita, his girl, increased every day. They, of course, still thought he was in jail. Perhaps they didn't even know whether he was alive! Could he write to them? But maybe they were no longer at the same addresses. So much could have happened while he was in jail. Perhaps it was better to leave them in the dark for the time being. Then they wouldn't worry. And when he did show up, their joy would be all the greater. But he couldn't stand to wait much longer; he was sick with longing.

One day, as he stood half hidden behind the hedge, staring down the country road to see whether Van Buren was coming yet, Mrs. Versteeg tapped on the window and motioned to him to come inside.

"I've saved you a nice cup of coffee," she told him as he came in. "Sit down and relax. I want to talk to you. You don't like it here, do you? Aren't we taking good care of you? Why don't you make things easier on us and stop being so restless? When you're at the table, all you do is stare out the window and hardly say a word. You spend half your time trotting down to the road and standing behind that hedge. You've been saved, I would say miraculously. Now don't let impatience make life miserable for you.

"You don't have to worry about Van Buren. He's doing all he can, I assure you. The man has a heart of gold. Yes, I know you're eager to see your mother, and you're worried whether she's all right. But all your worrying isn't going to do her a smidgen of good, is it? Maybe what's wrong is that you don't put your trust in God. Look, see that text under the clock?"

On the wall hung a text written in gilt letters on a black velvet background: "Cast all your cares on Him, for He cares for you."

"With all these Jews and divers hidden around the place I'd soon be overcome by uncertainty and fear too if I didn't keep reminding myself of that. No, you don't have to apologize. I can see we understand each other, you and I. Now give me your cup, and you go chop some wood for me. I've got some laundry that needs doing. And next time you feel down in the mouth, John, you come to me! Let me mother you a bit."

He cut wood and stoked up the fire. And then he put on an apron and helped Mrs. Versteeg wring out the clothes. Soon he was humming to himself. Thereafter, the days went considerably faster and seemed much less bleak. The old woman's words had reached deep into John's heart.

He also began to take an interest in his fellow fugitives. Two Jewish couples were housed in the haymow in a room made of straw bales. The only light they had was from a small skylight. In a small cubicle that Mr. Versteeg had built over the stable lived a law student. A former factory worker slept in the house because he passed for a farm hand and worked out in the fields with the farmer. He had gone into hiding when he had been ordered to report for work in Germany. The student had refused to sign a statement swearing loyalty to the Nazi administration. (*Most* students had refused to sign, and nearly all the universities had been closed down.)

The only person John saw during the day was the

farm hand. The student was studying for his law exams, which he hoped to take as soon as the war was over. The Jewish ladies whiled away the daylight hours reading or doing some handicraft or other. One of the men was studying lettering styles, and the other did minor repairs or wove baskets in the attic or in the shed.

But every evening at nine o'clock, everyone gathered in the stables, where a radio was concealed in one of the stalls underneath the manger. They all crowded around it, straining to hear the latest war news from England, sometimes holding their breath so that they wouldn't miss anything. Despite the interference from German jammers, they managed to catch almost all that was said.

The thing on everyone's mind was the invasion. How was it going? To hear that the Germans were being routed in Italy and that Rome had been taken by the Americans with little or no damage was, of course, great news! And so was the fact that after a time of regrouping, the Russians were now preparing an all-out offensive. But that was still far away. Normandy was close by. On the map it appeared to be right next door. One of the Jewish couples had spent several vacations in Normandy before the war.

When the Allies had first landed, everyone on the farm had thought that it would only be a matter of marching inland a few kilometers before they would all be liberated. But they had been disappointed. The Allies had to fight hard for every kilometer they advanced. But thousands of ships plied the channel day and night, bringing a constant stream of reinforcements and tanks and guns, while swarms of Allied planes bombed and strafed the German positions.

Soon, any day now, they told one another, the English and American forces would be strong enough to break through the German lines and then they would really begin moving. It would be only a couple of weeks before they would be in Paris and Brussels. And then it would be Holland's turn! The war would be over before winter, and their hard times would be over.

After the broadcast, they moved to the house; and behind tightly closed shutters and with the dog on guard outside, the discussion of the latest news went on until bedtime. The faces of the two Jewish couples shone with hope as they looked forward to the end of the war and made plans to rebuild their businesses. But the farmer was more down to earth. The Germans, he said, had invented a terrible new weapon, a rocket called the *V-1*. With it, they could bomb the English cities from launching pads in Belgium and Holland.

"Nothing can beat that!" he said. "A flying bomb that can cross the North Sea! Whatever you might say about them, those Germans are tough and smart." John, too, thought the *V-1* was an awesome invention. But Bob, the law student, was sure it would make little difference in the war.

"Sure, of course the Germans brag it up to high heaven! But they had to do something to pump the morale back into their troops. When the invasion came, they made a big hullabaloo because now they were going to show the world how quickly they'd shove the Allies back into the sea. But you don't hear any of them talking like that now!

"And about that *V-1*. Sure, some of them land in English cities like London, where they may destroy a couple of homes or even a whole block. It may even kill a handful of women and kids. That's horrible, but it won't win the war for the Germans. And they know it themselves. There's another weapon, however, which, if the Germans use it, will put an end to the war in just a few days."

"What? What kind of weapon?"

"I've got a picture of it upstairs," said Bob. "Wait a minute. I'll fetch it."

He returned in a couple of minutes with a poster-size sheet of paper. It was a drawing of a German soldier waving his rifle with a white flag tied to its bayonet. The caption read in German: THE LATEST WEAPON!

"Good work!" said John. "What are you going to do with it?"

"Someone will pick this up tomorrow, and within a week reproductions of it will be posted all over the country, especially close to German bars. It gives our uniformed German friends something to think about. Here's another one. Meant for our own workers, in case they're thinking of volunteering to work in Germany. The Germans are making them all kinds of fancy promises if they go."

At the door of the Labor Ministry stood a human figure with the head of an extremely dull-looking jackass. He was saying to himself, "I think I'll go to Germany too. They say the grass is much greener over there."

John suddenly saw the student through new eyes. He

was such a pale, slight, ineffectual-looking fellow; but in the loneliness of his little cubicle, he too was taking part in the fight for freedom.

Before they retired for the night, Bob and the two couples took a walk around the farm in the dusk of the summer evening, taking the dog with them to warn them of approaching strangers. John went back to his haystack. Overhead, the ominous drone of one formation of bombers after another headed east to continue their battering of the German cities.

About eleven o'clock the next morning, they passed over once again: formations of from twenty to thirty huge silvery birds high up in the sky. Swarming around them like quarreling wrens were the much smaller fighters. Full of awe, John and Mr. and Mrs. Versteeg watched the magnificent sight. Suddenly the dog barked a warning, as a pretty buggy pulled by two spotted ponies turned onto the farmyard from the dirt road.

"Oh, it's the lady," said Versteeg, doffing his cap.

A small gray woman threw down the reins and climbed down off the buggy with the help of the farmer. She motioned to John to fetch a suitcase and two tote bags stashed in the back of the buggy. John had already been told about her and knew why she was there. She had taken upon herself the duty of looking after the divers in the district. With her, she had new ration cards and a pile of new books for the Jewish ladies, and also the latest issues of the underground newspapers, FREE HOLLAND and TRUE. This time she also had a message for John, "Van Buren says to be patient a couple more days. They're having trouble getting the right seal for your papers."

"And I've got a suit for you in the suitcase," added the old lady. "Try it on for size while I go see how those poor dears are doing up in the haymow."

Mrs. Versteeg told John to use the bedroom. In the suitcase he found a fine used suit which almost fit him, except that it had to be taken in at the waist. Besides the suit, there were two beautiful shirts, two sets of underwear, a blue tie, a hat (also too large), several handkerchiefs, a razor, a pocket knife, a cigarette holder filled with cigarettes, and a wallet with twenty guilders in it. That wonderful old lady had put him back in circulation!

When she came back into the house, he had to model the suit for her, and she studied him from all sides. His thanks she waved away with an offhanded gesture.

"When the warden told me about you, I knew you didn't have a thing to call your own," she said. "Turn around once more. The pants should be shortened a little too. But Mrs. Versteeg or one of the other ladies can fix that. Right, Mrs. Versteeg? And let me see that hat a minute. Here, you just fold up a piece of newspaper, like this, and then tuck it inside the headband. Here, try it. See? Now it fits perfectly."

It was coffee time, so the lady joined them for a cup. She had some sensational news. A little over a week ago, on a Sunday afternoon, the underground had hit the detention center in Arnhem and freed more than fifty prisoners. Just think of it! In the middle of the day! The men who had been freed were all resistance fighters, some of whom had already been condemned to death.

The raiders had entered the prison through the quarters of the prison director; so the guards had no idea what was happening until they were looking down gun barrels. The guards were locked in the cells instead of the prisoners, and the fifty prisoners walked calmly out of the prison in small groups, quickly dispersing all over the city. Most of them immediately caught trains to other parts of the country.

"No one can understand better than you what that must have meant for those men," the old woman said to John. "I was so happy when I heard about it that I treated all the children in my neighborhood to fresh strawberries. The Germans must have been furious! They're not in the best mood as it is, with the invasion going so well. They're getting more vicious than ever. Same with the Dutch Nazis, the National Guard. Why, on the way over here that Geurtsen, the leader of the local National Guard—he stopped me on the road. 'What do you want?' I asked him. And then he said he was going to search my buggy. The nerve of that man!

" 'Geurtsen,' I said, 'you listen to me. When your mother was a girl, she used to be a maid in our villa. And one day she got very, very ill. Did she ever tell you about that? Well, if I hadn't nursed her then, you wouldn't be bothering me now. So move your carcass or I'll take my switch to you, you insolent whelp! And if you ever stop me again, I'll make you wish you hadn't when the war's over. And that's only a couple of months away. Understand?'

"Well, then of course he stepped aside, the spineless . . . ."

"But what would you have done if they had insisted?" cried Mrs. Versteeg. "That was a close call! You'd better be careful."

"He'd have rued the day if he had put his dirty hands on my buggy!" the old woman said coldly, her eyes glinting. "If necessary I've got something with me besides my whip." She snapped open her purse, checked inside, and closed it again. "The work has to go on, especially now that we're almost at the finish. No doubt you're eager to get back into action again. Right, young man?"

"Yes, ma'am," said John.

He was still turning his answer over in his mind when the buggy disappeared down the dirt road. Was he *really* eager to get back into it? Sure, when the lady told about the jailbreak, his heart glowed at the thought that poor and rich, young and old were still fighting side by side. And looking back on it, he would love to have been in on that raid. But that was only in looking back.

Whenever he was faced with such a dangerous task, he always dreaded it. Did others experience the same fear as he, or was he the only one? He had always helped because there was no other choice. It was his duty! That would probably happen again. Yes, he would have to join in the struggle again, he realized. He wouldn't be able to keep out of it. But Father was probably dead already, so he had to survive for the sake of Mother and the children. Eager? No, he was only eager to see Mother.

A couple of days later, the farmer butchered the pig, and at night, after listening to the news, everyone joined in preparing and canning the meat. A large tub stood hissing on the stove. Eshuis, the factory worker, was busy cleaning out the intestines, while the women treated the meat to make sausages. John helped the farmer salt down the pork. Everyone was in a good mood because they had just heard that the Americans had taken Cherbourg and that the Russians had launched their big offensive and were driving back the Germans along the whole eastern front.

"It won't be long," said Eshuis, "and we'll be putting Hitler and his bunch through the meat grinder."

"Oh, yuccch! Cut it out!" squealed Mrs. Versteeg, pulling a face and laughing at the same time.

Suddenly the dog started barking and voices sounded on the yard. The two Jewish couples rushed for the back door, but Versteeg called them back. He could tell by the way the dog was barking that the visitors were friends. A few seconds later, Van Buren and the game warden stepped into the kitchen. They both sniffed the air and licked their lips.

"Hmmm!" said Van Buren. "We've timed it just right. No wonder you've stayed here so long, John. You've found the ideal boarding house! Here you are. This is for you."

While the two men tasted a slice of blood sausage, John closely examined his new papers: an I.D. stamped with the Assen city seal, a German pass complete with official seals, a registration card, and the ration cards for the current period.

"Satisfactory?" asked Van Buren. "Then add a few grease spots, fray the corners a bit, and make them look old and used. You can leave tomorrow if you still want to. I can get you a ride to Zwolle. The warden is taking a patient to a hospital there."

"I can pick you up at eight," said the game warden.

"Or have you changed your mind?" asked Van Buren. "You know you're welcome here. Right, Mrs. Versteeg?"

"Oh, he's not going to stay here," she said. "You couldn't keep him here with a team of horses."

She was right. John was too excited to sleep that night. At eight o'clock he had been peering down the country road for some time already. His suitcase was all packed. But Mrs. Versteeg made him open it again so she could put in a couple of sausages and a piece of bacon for his mother.

Still, it was hard for him to say goodbye, and the Versteegs made him promise that he would come back to see them after the war. When he left with the warden, the old couple stood beside the hedge, waving, until he was out of sight.

"Where would the underground be without such simple, courageous people?" he thought. "Opening their home and risking their lives for all kinds of strangers."

"The underground . . . . Yes," he thought with a sudden pain; he was once again thinking of himself as part of the underground.

CHAPTER TWO

John made the trip to Zwolle in a car equipped with a converter, the only car left in the entire village. A local mechanic had fastened a heavy iron cylinder on the back of the car, which produced methane gas by cooking wood. But the gas produced in this way enabled the car to go no faster than forty kilometers per hour.

A sick woman lay in the back, with a nurse sitting beside her. Her husband sat beside the driver. John sat on the front fender with the headlight between his legs, scanning the sky for Allied fighters. It was a cloudless summer day, so the car would be visible to airplanes many kilometers away. John had a cool spot for his ride; he got a little support from the hood of the old Ford, and he could hang on to the headlight. Every fifteen minutes or so they had to stop to stoke up the converter, and John got a chance to stretch his legs.

At one place where they stopped, a large gang of men were busy digging deep holes at regular intervals along the road—foxholes for the Germans in case there was fighting here. Only a few men were actually digging; the rest were leaning on their shovels or talking. They were working against their will, one of the men told John. They didn't want to help the Germans in their fight against the Allies, but they had no choice. At first, of five hundred men who had been called up from a nearby town, only thirty had reported.

"So then the Germans burned down the homes of several of the fellows who didn't show up," said the man, "and now they've got three hundred volunteers. What else could we do? They might have burned the whole town. But just wait! We'll get our turn soon enough!"

Otherwise, the trip was uneventful. Only once did they hear the whine of fighters, but at the time they were on a stretch of road overshadowed by huge trees. When they came out from under the trees, the sky was clear again.

John said goodbye at the hospital, and then, carrying his little suitcase, he walked across town to the railroad station. For the first time in many months he was strolling along among the people as a free man, and although it made him feel very vulnerable, he enjoyed it nevertheless. He noticed a few changes that had come about during his imprisonment. Real bicycle tires seemed to have disappeared, and everyone had to make do with substitutes. Some used a section of garden hose, and a few even went clattering along the pavement on the bare rims. Shop windows were virtually empty. One shoe store was selling nothing but wooden sandals, and a tailor's shop had a sign in the window: "Have extra cloth? We'll convert it into a cap."

In front of a butcher shop, a big mob had gathered. A policeman stood by the shop door to keep order. A large sign in the window announced: "Meat for sale without ration cards this afternoon." An open truck was just making its way into the lane beside the store. On the back lay a dead horse.

"There it comes," some of the people in the crowd shouted. "Hurry up with it, or else the war will be over before we get our turn." Everyone laughed and hooted, and more wisecracks followed.

John bought a ticket to Assen and was told that a train would be leaving in a half hour. As he was going through the station check, he saw two German soldiers pacing by on the platform, and for a moment he got a panicky, trapped feeling. "Relax," he told himself. "Your papers are in good shape and those soldiers are regular army. All they know about is fighting other soldiers."

To prove to himself that he wasn't afraid, he followed the soldiers into the waiting room and ordered a cup of coffee. But it was such a tasteless brew he didn't even finish it. Time for him to get out on the platform, for it was quickly starting to fill with people. Nevertheless, the train didn't come rolling into the station until a full hour later. Pulling the long row of cars was a small locomotive that shuddered and groaned under its heavy burden. The best equipment had been hauled off to Germany.

All the coaches were crammed with people, except the

one immediately behind the engine. People avoided the first car because, whenever a train was strafed, the engine was what the fighter pilot was aiming at, but the nearest car often got hit too. The last coach on the train was also empty. A sign on its doors said, "Reserved for Military Personnel." Behind it were a number of boxcars also filled with people.

The train was mobbed even before it came to a complete stop, and John found himself being swept aboard. He was shoved and elbowed from all sides, as well as being roundly cursed by a man who barked his shins on John's suitcase. Finally, he found himself standing in a corridor, tightly pressed on all sides by a sweating mass of people, and holding his suitcase over his head. His toes ached because someone had stepped on them with wooden clogs.

"This is crazy," he thought to himself. "I'm almost suffocating already." With a great deal of difficulty, he managed to extricate himself from the crowded coach. Back on the platform, he walked to the front of the train and boarded the first coach. Several other people had also decided to sacrifice safety for the sake of comfort, and John had to do a bit of looking to find an empty seat.

He hung his coat on a hook by the window, wiped his forehead and neck, and dug into his suitcase for the sandwiches that Mrs. Versteeg had packed for him. They were homemade bread with homemade summer sausage. As he bit into his sandwich, he noticed the eyes of his fellow passengers fixed on him. It almost made him lose his appetite.

"My, my," said the lady sitting across from him with a skinny child on her lap, "where are you from? It's been a long time since we've seen anything like that in Amsterdam. Things seem to be a lot better wherever you come from."

"I'm just returning from a visit to relatives on the farm," he explained, "and they butchered just before I left. Would you like a sandwich too?" Once he had started handing them out, however, it was impossible to stop. There wasn't a person aboard who wasn't hungry. Finally, all John had left was the sandwich he had already started. No matter; he had been well fed the last few weeks, and he could travel on his reserves for a while.

"Once in a while I've been able to get an extra loaf of bread on top of our ration," the woman told him. "But lately the baker has been charging five guilders a loaf. There's no way we can pay that. So I'm taking our youngest to my sister's in Meppel. If there's plenty to eat around there, maybe I'll stay too."

The passengers went on about food shortages and about the outrageous prices being charged on the black market. One man had paid eighty guilders for an ounce of tea. And another, two hundred guilders for a set of bicycle tires. The first day after he had put them on his bike, the Germans had appropriated it.

"Blasted thieves!" he said.

The woman and child got out at Meppel, and no other passengers took their places. But when the train was already moving, a short fat man came puffing up beside the coach and at the very last minute caught the railing by the door and pulled himself aboard. He was bald, but he had a young, expressive face with squinting eyes. John guessed him to be about forty years old.

"Just made it," he panted, laughing. "This must be my lucky day." Then he gave the salute of the Dutch Nazi party and shouted, "Huzzah, Comrades!"

The faces in the coach became expressionless. No one responded.

"No members of the N.S.M. present?" asked the man. "Good, then we know what's what, right? I'm no Nazi either, but I like to know who I'm traveling with. My name is Vos: *V* for victory; *O* for orange; and *S* for sly, because those who aren't strong have to be sly. Glad to meet you all."

He tossed his briefcase into the rack overhead and took the seat kitty-corner from John.

"Hey, you know, I was just reading the want ads, and I saw one of those man-wants-to-meet-woman ads. It said, 'Gentleman with half pound of coffee wants to meet lady with two pounds of sugar. Object: sweet matrimony.' Marriages have been founded on less, right?"

The whole coach was laughing, and everyone relaxed.

"Does anybody know the one about the discharged mental patient? Great! This guy had been locked up for five years, see? But finally he was declared sane.

"He comes into town and says to himself, 'First I'm going to get me a bite to eat.' He's got a ten-guilder goldpiece in his wallet from before the time he was committed. So he walks into this restaurant.

" 'Give me a whiskey,' he says.

" 'All we have is black market whiskey,' says the waiter.

" 'Must be a new kind,' thinks the man. But when the waiter comes back with the bottle, it's just as white as always.

"He doesn't understand it, but it tastes great! So he orders a steak.

" 'Do you have ration cards?' asks the waiter. No, he doesn't have any; he doesn't even know what they are!

" 'Should I bring you a black market steak then, sir?' asks the waiter.

" 'Fine,' says the man. But the steak isn't a bit black.

" 'Either this waiter is crazy or I am,' the man thinks to himself.

"Afterward, he asks for the bill and almost loses his teeth when he sees it: thirty guilders!

" 'All I've got is this ten-guilder goldpiece,' he tells the waiter.

" 'That's fine sir,' says the waiter, and he gives the man twenty guilders in change.

"The fellow walks out of the restaurant and promptly recommits himself. He doesn't know that a ten-guilder goldpiece is worth over fifty guilders nowadays."

Mr. Vos's jokes soon had the whole coach in a jovial mood. He seemed to have a limitless repertoire of amusing anecdotes about the war. At the next stop the man sitting opposite John got off, and Mr. Vos slid over to sit across from him. They were both looking out the window when two men came out of the station onto the platform. One was wearing a German uniform and carrying a briefcase under his arm; the other was dressed in civilian clothes. They strode along the train and climbed in a couple of cars down.

"What are they doing *here*?" one of the passengers asked. "You'd think they'd ride in the special coach reserved for Germans."

But Vos appeared to know what was going on.

"S.D. check," he said. He seemed uneasy about the presence of the German security police on the train, for he stood up, got his briefcase from the rack and went to the door. He stuck out his head as if he meant to get off, but then he seemed to think better of it and came back to his seat. He slid the briefcase under his seat, dug a newspaper out of his pocket and concealed himself behind it.

"RACE AND NATION," John read on the masthead—the paper of the Dutch Nazi party, the National Socialist Movement. He noticed the other passengers eyeing the man uneasily. Was he a bad one after all? Had he courted their friendship in order to betray them? They all tried to recall whether they had said anything treasonous.

The train wheezed on across the spacious countryside of Drenthe, John's home province. Here and there John recognized places where he had rambled about with Father or Fritz. He was enjoying the feeling of coming home and had almost forgotten about the S.D. inspectors when suddenly they came barging in. A chill went down his back. There they were! Once again he was face to face with the enemy. Now he would see how good Van Buren's papers were.

"I.D.'s please," said one of them.

John took his I.D. from his wallet and also got out his German pass. He waited. His nervousness was suddenly displaced by a strength and confidence that came from somewhere outside of himself, as it had so many times before, and he felt as if nothing could harm him now. This happened every time he found himself confronted with danger, but each time it surprised him. The man in civilian clothes had bright, alert eyes. He held out his hand, and John gave him his I.D. The man studied it from all sides, gave John a long, hard stare, and handed the card back without a word. Then he turned to John's jolly companion.

But Mr. Vos had fallen asleep. His head lolled against the wall, and he snored audibly. *Race and Nation* dangled from his limp hand with the masthead toward the aisle. In his lapel was the red pin of the N.S.M. So he was a Nazi after all! Or . . .?

But it seemed to make no difference to the S.D. inspectors. The uniformed German shook him by the shoulder and demanded to see his I.D. Yawning, Mr. Vos handed over his card, holding out his hand to take it back.

The civilian inspector studied the card closely and whispered to the German officer, showing him the card. Then he turned to face Mr. Vos. "This I.D. has been tampered with," he said sternly.

"Don't make me laugh!" said Mr. Vos. "Are you sure your eyes haven't been tampered with?" But John could see fear in his eyes.

"Are you a member of the N.S.M.?"

"See for yourself."

"Can I see your membership card?"

"I'm sorry, I don't happen to have it on me. I had to turn it in for a minor correction."

"Yes, of course. Do you have any luggage with you?"

"No."

"Then who does that briefcase belong to?" The inspector pointed under the seat with the toe of his shoe.

"A briefcase?" Mr. Vos looked down under the seat and looked up, feigning surprise. "That's the first time I've seen it."

"Does that belong to you?" the man asked John.

John hesitated a moment. He realized that his fellow passenger was in a bind, but he could hardly claim the briefcase as his without knowing what was in it.

"My suitcase is on the rack right above me," he said.

The S.D. officer grabbed the briefcase, dug around in it and triumphantly produced a thick wad of ration cards.

"What a coincidence!" said the inspector mockingly. "A falsified I.D., a party card that happens to be elsewhere, and a briefcase full of ration cards which got under your seat all by itself. Don't *you* think that's quite a coincidence?"

Mr. Vos had turned deathly pale. All his bravado and cleverness were gone. The S.D. in civilian clothes held his wrists while the uniformed man snapped handcuffs on him. John was breathing fast. A man's life might be at stake. Wasn't there anything he could do?

"Come along!" said the German pulling Mr. Vos by the handcuffs.

"Now you," snapped the other man to John. "Open your suitcase."

At that moment the train braked so hard that half the passengers were thrown from their seats. The steam whistle screamed as if in terror, and the wheels screeched on the tracks. Above the noise from the train and the shrieks of terrified people came the howl of airplane engines.

"Air attack! Fighters! Out, out!" people were shouting. The doors were jerked open, and bodies were tumbling out before the train had even stopped. The Germans were two of the first ones out.

"To the other side!" shouted John, grabbing Mr. Vos, who had tumbled into the aisle. He pushed the man ahead of him, grabbing his suitcase. Then he stepped on a briefcase and scooped that up too. A woman fell over him as he bent over. She screamed and kicked, but John scrambled free, still clutching the briefcase. Mr. Vos was turning the handle of the train door with his manacled hands. John threw himself against him, and they both spilled out of the train and rolled down the embankment just as the machine guns of the English fighters began chattering. Fragments of fire and metal spattered in all directions. Everywhere people were screaming and moaning. The planes sheared low over the train and seemed to swallow the screams of terror in their own voracious roar. Mr. Vos lay in the ditch sobbing, tears coursing down his cheeks. But John pulled him up.

"Go man!" he yelled. "Run! Move, you're free!"

John shoved him up the other side of the ditch, over a fence, and into a field. They ran for a row of bushes and

trees that crossed the field at right angles to the railway tracks. Behind them, the locomotive shrieked like a dying animal. Again the planes came diving low for another attack, their guns blazing directly above them.

As they ran through a gap in the trees, a loud hissing behind them told them that the locomotive had been hit and was spouting steam. But they ran on, skirting an apple orchard, through another windbreak, and across a pasture. The cows scattered in all directions, their tails high in the air. On the other side of the pasture, Mr. Vos snagged himself on a barbed-wire fence. He twisted around and with trembling fingers carefully began freeing the fabric of his pants.

"*Tear* it loose, you fool!" yelled John. "Come on, we've got to keep going!"

"I can't go any farther," Vos said, panting, almost blubbering. But John yanked him to his feet and pushed the fat little man ahead of him. Now they were on a little trail winding between clumps of alders.

"Keep going, man! You're running for your life!"

John prodded him on until they had struggled through some dense brush and come to the edge of a swamp, where the man collapsed on the grass. John dropped down beside him, wiped the sweat off his face, and remained sitting awhile to catch his breath. Everything was quiet behind them. The planes had gone. What was happening back at the train? The two S.D. officers would be looking for their prisoner, of course. How far had they come? It couldn't be much farther than two kilometers.

"My hat," thought John. "I left my hat on the train.

Oh well, who needs a hat in beautiful weather like this? It was too big anyway. And I managed to keep this funny little man out of the clutches of the Germans."

"What do you say, Mr. Vos?" said John happily. "Bet you didn't expect this when those S.D. goons picked you up! Aren't you thankful those planes came when they did? Things didn't look too good for you back there."

But Mr. Vos just lay back gasping for air and didn't say anything for a while. Finally, he held up his hands and looked at his handcuffs. "What . . . what am I going to do about these?" he said worriedly. "I can't show myself anywhere wearing these things, can I?"

"He's actually a pitiful character," John thought, looking at the puffy red face streaked with tears and sweat. "You meet all kinds in the underground."

He crawled over to the man and pulled his handkerchief out of his breast pocket. "Here, let me wipe your face a minute. You're covered with dust. Don't give up! So far we've been doing beautifully. We've got to get going again, but don't worry, I know my way around here. Just leave it to me!"

What to do about the handcuffs, however, John had no idea.

"Look, I even managed to grab your briefcase. I hope the ration cards are still in it."

"That isn't my briefcase."

"What?"

"No, that inspector took mine."

"The one in the uniform?"

"No, the other one."

John grinned. The one in civilian clothes had also been carrying a briefcase. And, of course, he had put it down when he was putting the handcuffs on Mr. Vos. Quickly, John snapped open the latch and laughed aloud in delight. It was indeed the German's briefcase. He pulled out some papers.

"Look, it's all S.D. stuff! Sheets with the S.D. letterhead, forms, and what's this? Dossier of Overman, Karl. Probably a transcript of someone's interrogation. We'll have to take a good look at this later on. And some newspapers. Hey, look at this: it looks like a diary or an appointment book. That might be important! Sandwiches and a piece of bratwurst. Aha! Just what we need!"

John pulled a heavy service revolver from the bottom of the briefcase. It was a beauty, he could tell at a glance. His hands shook a little as he checked to see whether it was loaded. Sure enough, it had a full clip! Then he looked up into the large, frightened eyes of Mr. Vos, and he burst out laughing. He jumped up. He was so pleased, he could have danced with glee. He had spit in the enemy's eye and gotten away with it.

"Pretty good swap, wouldn't you say, Mr. Vos? This makes me feel a whole lot better!"

He slid the gun into his pants pocket, opened his suitcase, and put the briefcase inside.

"Let's go," he said to his companion. "No need to look behind us. They won't find us anymore. Besides, if they do, we're no longer defenseless."

So they marched on, skirting the swamp and cutting across meadows and marshlands. It was a perfect summer day, and John was back in the familiar terrain of his youth. Around them were the purple bell heather, the blue gentians, and the reddish-purple loosestrife. Fireweeds, Uncle Gerrit called them. That's right! He wasn't far from good old Uncle Gerrit's little house. After he had found some help for the fat little fellow beside him, he would look up Uncle Gerrit. Why was Mr. Vos looking so down in the mouth?

"Too bad about those ration cards," said John, trying to comfort him a little. "Did they need them real bad?"

"Who?"

"Well, the people you were talking to. You're helping to supply divers aren't you?"

"Yes, yes, of course," said Mr. Vos. "I really should have had a lot more of them. But now they'll have to do the best they can in Groningen. If only these bloody cuffs were off!"

He jerked at them in frustration and winced as they bit into his wrists.

"And I don't have an I.D. anymore either," he added glumly.

"What was wrong with your I.D. anyway?" asked John.

"Oh, I'm thirty-eight, born in 1906. I figured I wouldn't be drafted to work in Germany if I were over forty, so I changed the date to 1896."

"You didn't do that yourself, did you?"

"Sure! It wasn't so difficult. You could hardly tell."

"That was stupid!" said John. "How come you didn't let someone do it who knew what he was doing?

What else did you have in the briefcase? Anything dangerous? Did you make any notes?"

"Notes?"

"Yes, like addresses of other workers. Or don't you write anything down?"

"No, not me. I've got all my addresses in my head."

"Good, that's the best way," said John. "Never write anything down if you can help it."

At last they came to a narrow dirt road. In the distance, they could see the red tiles of a farmhouse jutting above a grove of trees.

"Sssh! Listen."

The sound of wagon wheels came squeaking down the road. A horse snorted.

"Into the ditch! Quick!" said John.

Mr. Vos disappeared into the high weeds, and John walked ahead to meet the wagon. A young farmer came into sight riding on a battered old tipcart. When he saw John, he slid his straw hat back on his head and reined in his horse.

"Well, well," he said looking down at John, "how did such a fine-looking gentleman with a suitcase get way out here among us mud farmers?"

He spoke in the dialect of Drenthe, and John replied in the same idiom.

"If clothes make a gentleman," he answered laughing. "The train wasn't in any shape to go on."

"Oh, you got here from the railroad, eh? I heard the planes a while back. I wondered who those limeys were shooting at."

"Yeah, the train has had it. Let me ask you

something. Do folks around here have much truck with the Nazis?"

"What you want to know is, do I belong to the N.S.M., right?" He looked at John and spat on the road. "I'll excuse you for asking, since you're a stranger around here. Otherwise, I'd take your question as an insult."

"Glad to hear it," said John. "Well, then, here's your chance to do a good deed. I want you to meet somebody I took with me from the train. Don't worry. He's harmless."

He shouted to Mr. Vos to come out of the ditch, and then he began to tell the farmer what had happened. But as Mr. Vos came scrambling up out of the tall grass, the farmer interrupted him.

"Me help that guy? You gotta be kidding! Look what he's got on his jacket."

On the lapel of Mr. Vos's suitcoat was the N.S.M. pin that he had put on in the train. John had forgotten all about it. He reached over and pulled it off.

"It doesn't mean a thing, I assure you. He only put it on to throw off the Germans, but it didn't work. They picked him up with a briefcase full of ration cards. He was being dragged off to jail. That's why the handcuffs. Here, you can have the pin. It'd make a pretty nose ring for one of your pigs."

"No thanks. It'd probably spoil the meat," said the young farmer chuckling. "But you can thank God you got such a break. That sure is a pretty set of bracelets. You sure you want them off, Mr.? Seems a shame. You'll need a blacksmith, I should think. But how are we going to get you over there?"

"Can the man be trusted?" asked John.

"Tell you what! I'll take your word about this guy, if you'll take my word about our blacksmith."

"Done!"

"Fine. I reckon I can trust your word. Hop aboard, both of you. You caught me at a bad time, but first things first, I guess."

He drove the tipcart into a nearby field, where they helped Mr. Vos into the cart and covered him with a heap of dry branches that had been stacked there for firewood. The suitcase they buried with him. John climbed into the seat beside the farmer. The village was a half hour down the road, and they met no one until they were almost there. Apparently school had just let out, for they suddenly met groups of children walking along the road. Almost every one of them was carrying an orange.

"Hi, Dad!" shouted two little girls. "Hey! Where you going?"

"I've got to stop at the bakery a minute," the farmer shouted back. "You hurry home and tell Mother to start with the milking."

"They get them oranges from the teacher every now and again," he explained to John. "Our Nazi mayor buys them for the kids. Sometimes he gives them little bottles of pills to take home too. Fightermints, he calls 'em."

"You mean vitamins?" said John.

"Yeah, that's what I said. What do they need that kind of stuff for? The mayor, he says it's for their health. But they ain't sick. We can look after our own kids without those Nazis butting in. Maybe they're trying to poison 'em or something. So I sez to my kids, you toss 'em over the fence into the mayor's yard. If they're supposed to be so all-fired good, let him eat 'em himself. He'll need 'em soon enough when the Allies lock him up!"

John grinned to himself: a typical Drenthe farmer, he thought, a hard-headed firebrand.

The blacksmith was a friendly fellow with a big bushy mustache. He was busy making horseshoes out of an old piece of angle iron. New iron was no longer available. He seemed happy to drop what he was doing and tackle something different. The farmer didn't have to do much talking to persuade him to help.

He led his horse and wagon into his shop and closed the doors behind them. A few minutes later, they had Mr. Vos dug out from underneath the load of branches, and they took him into the blacksmith's house. The smith wore out two files cutting through the hard metal of the handcuffs. Meanwhile, the farmer backed the wagon out of the shop to take the load of branches over to the bakery.

"Will I see you again sometime?" he asked John at the door. "I can tell by the way you talk you're from around here. From Assen, you say. Well, if you ever need any help again, Eising's the name—Job Eising."

The blacksmith's wife had the coffee poured when John came back in. Mr. Vos sat rubbing his wrists for a while, but soon he was back to his old self again. He gave a dramatic account of what had happened on the train, making it sound as if he had been utterly fearless throughout. Then he once more dipped into his great repository of jokes. The blacksmith made the house reverberate with his laughter. Without being asked, he suddenly offered to help Mr. Vos out of his awkward situation. He could stay there, at least for the time being, and the smith would see to it that he got a new I.D. He knew where to go, he said. John could stay too if he wanted to.

"Thank you, but I'd like to go on as soon as possible," said John.

"Where you headed? To Assen? There are no more busses coming through tonight."

"Do you think I might be able to borrow or rent a bike somewhere?"

"You can use one of ours," said the blacksmith generously. "I'll give you my wife's. Just try to get it back as soon as possible. But you're not leaving until you've had something to eat!"

John was lift alone in the room with Mr. Vos for a while. "Listen," he said. "I'd rather you didn't say anything about the briefcase and the revolver, okay? A little while ago I thought you were going to spill everything."

"Why not?" asked Mr. Vos, looking puzzled.

"Because!" said John brusquely. "Because it isn't necessary. The fewer people that know of something, the less chance of being given away."

"Okay, okay," replied Mr. Vos, a little huffily. "Spare me your sermons. You resistance guys make a big deal of everything."

"You resistance guys? You're in the resistance yourself, aren't you?"

"Yes, but not very long," he said grinning. "I still have to get used to the idea."

"Yes, that was pretty obvious today!" John said. "Maybe you'd be . . . ." The blacksmith's wife interrupted him to tell them that supper was ready.

The sun was low on the horizon when John tied his suitcase onto the rear carrier of his borrowed bike. He was overjoyed to find that it still had prewar tires and tubes.

"If you get a flat, just keep pedaling," said the blacksmith. "Those tires aren't much good no more nohow. Have a safe trip! To get to Assen, you turn right after you get out of town."

"Thanks a *lot* for all your help," said John. "I'll get the bike back to you as soon as I can."

As he rode away, Mr. Vos stood by the window and made a *V* signal, at the same time giving John a broad wink. "He's sure a queer duck!" thought John.

He pedaled down main street and then looked back. The blacksmith was still watching. So he turned right as the man had instructed. But then he circled around the church and went back the way he had come, passing behind the blacksmith's shop. On the other side of town, he quickly found the bicycle trail that led through a provincial forest to the canal along which Uncle Gerrit lived. Suddenly he found himself pedaling for all he was worth. It seemed as if he could smell home and as if everything depended on his getting there before nightfall.

CHAPTER THREE

John was walking along the canal, pushing his bike. The rear tire had gone flat. Although the blacksmith had told him to ignore it and ride on, he thought it would be a shame to ruin the tire. The man had been so generous. If possible, he would like to return the bike in the same condition he had got it. If he moved right along, he should be able to reach Uncle Gerrit's place before the ten o'clock curfew. After curfew no one was allowed on the road except those with special permits.

The bike wobbled along on its flat. A pale moon reflected in the smooth black water of the canal. It probably wouldn't get much darker during the short summer night. Far in the distance sounded the rumble of English bombers. It seemed only to accentuate the stillness of the evening along the canal.

This was a very lonely stretch of road. John could hear the squeaking of a bicycle coming down the road behind him. Whoever it was didn't have his light on. It was still not too dark to see the road. John could hear the cyclist humming to himself. Suddenly, he stopped. He must have seen John. Slowly he pulled up beside him and said, "Good evening," coasting a bit beyond.

"Good evening," replied John. That voice . . . and that short, broad figure . . . . The man stopped and dismounted. When John saw *how* he dismounted, letting the bike slip forward out from between his legs and then catching it by the saddle, he knew for sure! The stocky figure waited for John to catch up.

"Got a flat?" he asked.

"Yeah, Fritz," John said in a hoarse voice. "How are you doing, brother?"

The other figure straightened up and took a step forward. "No! No, it can't be! John? John, is that you?" His bike clattered to the road, and the usually undemonstrative Fritz leaped at his brother and threw his arms about him sobbing like a child. Then he took John by the shoulders and shook him, pummeled him, pinched his cheeks, and pulled his hair.

"John, Johnny boy, is it really you?"

"It is, if you don't pull me apart first," said John.

A couple more sobs, a deep breath, and Fritz was back in control of himself. He picked up his bike.

"We thought you were dead," he explained. "William was here less than a week ago. He got the news from a guard in Amsterdam, who said you had been shipped out with a group of prisoners who were to be shot!"

"Did you tell Mom?"

"No, just Uncle Gerrit. I didn't dare tell Mom. She's

so . . . well, she isn't . . . . She's on a farm not far from Assen."

"Come on, Fritz, tell me! What's wrong with her?"

"Oh, nothing really. She was just so sure that you'd be back. She keeps talking about you. But how . . . ?"

"I escaped. It was a miracle that I made it. But I'll tell you about it some other time. Shh! Not so loud. Tell me, how is . . . are the others?"

How is Rita, he had meant to say, but her name stuck in his throat. What if something had happened to her?

"Everybody's doing fine. Tricia almost got caught a few days ago, but she's pretty slick, our sister. She can talk her way out of anything. And Uncle Gerrit is getting younger every day—now that the Germans are getting a pasting! I'm just on my way over there now. He's expecting us."

"Us?"

"Yeah, there's a group of us. You'll meet the others. Why don't you jump on the back and pull your bike along behind."

"Why don't I pedal?"

"Okay. Man, I'm still shaking! You louse, you gave me such a start! I couldn't believe my eyes!"

John laughed. It was still the same old Fritz, his little brother. Little? He had shoulders like a wrestler. It was hard work pedaling with such a load on the back. Ouch! Fritz was pinching and pounding on him again.

"Cut it out, Fritz, or we'll end up in the canal!"

"I can't help it! I still can't believe it's you. Man, did I feel sick when William . . . . It sure is great to have you back!"

Out of sheer joy, John stood up on the pedals and went swerving down the road as fast as he could with Fritz laughing on the back. But at the beginning of the path that led across the field to Uncle Gerrit's little house, John stopped and they got off the bike. John was thinking of Rita again. He took a deep breath.

"Fritz, before we go in, there's one more thing I've got to know."

"Yeah?"

"You didn't tell me about everyone."

"I didn't?"

"You know who I mean!"

"Me? I haven't the foggiest."

Was that blasted kid giggling?

"Come on—Rita! Have you heard anything about Rita?"

Now Fritz laughed out loud.

"You're still the same old square. It's no shame to be in love. I've got a girl myself, and I'm not afraid to let everyone know. You'll meet her pretty soon. She's nice. And gutsy! Why once . . . ."

"Fritz! Come on!"

"I'm sorry, John. But there's nothing to worry about. She's hiding in Friesland. Uncle Gerrit knows where she is. She's been here a couple of times already."

"Rita?"

"Who *else* are we talking about? She's looking great!"

It seemed as if a great load dropped from his shoulders. He had lost quite a bit of sleep in the last few weeks worrying about Mother and Rita. All for nothing, it seemed. He remembered Mrs. Versteeg's little talk: "Cast all your cares on Him." It was one text that he would never forget.

They walked down the path in single file, Fritz repeatedly turning around to tell John something else. It was almost as if he were afraid to let John out of his sight in case he would disappear again. But as they entered the shadows of the big oaks around the house, John told Fritz to be quiet a minute.

"What should we do now?" John asked quietly.

"What do you mean?"

"Should we go in together? Or should you go ahead?"

"Why?"

"Well, that old man, he's liable to get a heart attack when . . . ."

A voice interrupted them from the shadow of a nearby tree, "That old man isn't so easily shocked. He's had plenty of preparation. I could hear you two before you were halfway down the path."

"Uncle Gerrit!" cried John.

"How you doing, Johnny boy," said Uncle Gerrit. He seemed to swallow some tobacco. He coughed and hacked and blew his nose. "Well," he said in a strange voice, "my heart must be pretty sound. It told me you were still alive, and here you are . . . . My boy, my boy, how I prayed for you—for you and your father."

"Have you heard something from him?" John asked eagerly.

"I'll tell you more in a minute. They seem to be dragging him from one camp to the other. You'd better come in first."

"Anyone else here?" asked Fritz.

"Just Steve. We'll send him outside to keep watch. What do we call you, John?"

"John. John De Jong."

The inside of the little house was lit by a kerosene lamp, and from a pot standing on the stove, hissing and burping, came the smell of coffee. A young fellow with a round face and ruddy cheeks sat at the table reading something.

"Hello!" he said, rising.

"This is John De Jong," said Uncle Gerrit, introducing John. "You know Fritz. How'd you like to take over the watch outside for awhile Steve? When someone comes up the path, you ask, who is it? And you know the password: 'I've come to finish the coffee.' If anyone doesn't know the password, you holler—and you holler loud. Okay?"

"Yes, Uncle Gerrit."

"What about the coffee?" asked Fritz. "Is it ready yet?"

"In a minute, you caffein hound!"

Uncle Gerrit waited until Steve had gone out and shut the door behind him. Then he said, "Let's get our stories straight. The rest of the group is going to be here any minute. I don't think we ought to tell them who John is and how he got here. We've known these fellows for only a short while. It takes only one loose tongue to do you in. Right?"

"Yes. Fine, Uncle Gerrit. My I.D. says I'm a baker in Assen."

"Okay, that's how we'll introduce you. Now let me

get a good look at you in the light. Man, you're looking good!"

"But *you've* changed, Uncle Gerrit. You look so pale!"

"That's *your* doing. I guess I *am* getting old. Seeing you here in the flesh has got me all flustered. I've got chills running up and down my spine. Shh! Someone's coming! Remember, Fritz, this is the first time you've seen him. No slip-ups. Oh, we'll have to warn Vander May. Come in, gentlemen!"

Three young men dressed like farmers came into the room, blinking in the lamplight. They introduced themselves as George, Jack, and Arend. They looked John over carefully. And John noticed that George, a fellow about twenty years old with intelligent gray eyes, looked from him to Fritz and back again several times. John himself had never felt that he looked much like Fritz, but a stranger might notice a family resemblance.

"The only one still missing is Vander May," said Uncle Gerrit. "De Jong, will you spell Steve outside? You know the password."

"Smart move, Uncle Gerrit," John said to himself. This way he would be out of sight and wouldn't be asked any questions. He would also be able to intercept Vander May. Outside John found Steve lying in the grass under the oak trees.

"Uncle Gerrit wants you inside," he said. "I'm to take your place."

"Fine," drawled Steve and slowly picked himself up.

John followed the path toward the road a short way and then sat down in the tall grass along the canal. The grass was starting to get wet with dew, but the night was still mild. In the vast blackness of the sky, the stars were clearly visible. If only the war were over now, he would be completely happy.

Was that someone coming down the path? He sensed it more than he saw it. Now he could hear the hiss and whirr of bicycle tires, and he could just make out a dark silhouette. John jumped up.

"Who's there?" he called.

"What the . . . ! Man, you scared the daylights out of me!" rumbled a deep voice. "Just another coffee drinker. And who are you?"

"Can't you guess?"

"If I didn't know better, I'd say . . . ."

"Well, just pretend you *don't* know better, Mr. Vander May," said John, laughing. "You know me, all right!"

"John? John! How is it possible?"

"I'll tell you later. Listen, Mr. Vander May, you've never seen me before. My name is John De Jong."

"Is that necessary?"

"It's Uncle Gerrit's idea."

"Oh, well, then it's fine with me. John! Man, what a surprise! How did you get out here?"

"I'll tell you all about it later, Mr. Vander May. I escaped."

"No need to call me Mr. anymore. I'm hiding, just like yourself. Call me Josh, like all the others do. Is everyone here?"

"I think so."

"Good! Then we can begin. You've come at just the

right time! It's my job to organize a strike squad in this area. We need some men and organization here. Things are moving, John. It won't be long. Where should I put my bike?"

"Over here, in the woodshed," said John. At the same time, he thought to himself, "Will I be forced back into action? So soon?"

When he led Vander May into the house, Uncle Gerrit was just pouring coffee. He also put a plate of sliced coffee cake on the table.

"Help yourselves, boys! I baked it myself, especially for this occasion," he said. "You can take my chair, Josh."

"Where will *you* sit?"

"We need someone on watch outside."

"Maybe, but I'd like you to stay, Uncle Gerrit," said Vander May. "But all the others should be here too."

John stood up, seeing a chance to slip out.

"No, not you!" said Vander May and Uncle Gerrit with one voice.

"Who's armed?" asked Vander May. "Hands up. Fritz, John, George . . . and myself. That's . . . oh, you too, Steve? Okay, that's fine. We can risk it without a guard."

"Maybe so. But I'd still like a warning if we're going to get into a gunfight," said Uncle Gerrit, going to the door. "I'll be back in a minute."

They sat back to enjoy their coffee. Steve slurped. George winked at John. He nodded to Steve and made a fist, as if to say, he may look like a slow one, but he's a fighter! John looked at Steve again. Steve rubbed his nose and grinned as Uncle Gerrit came back in.

"Well, what did you do, Uncle Gerrit?"

"Oh, I had a couple of posts lying around, and I set them into shallow holes on each side of the path. On top of each pole I put a milk can and then strung a piece of clothes line between them. If anyone comes down the path, he'll pull over the poles and make enough noise to raise the dead. Maybe he'll even get beaned by one of the posts!"

When everyone had stopped laughing, suddenly Steve began, which touched off everyone else once more. But then Vander May called them to order. He paused a minute until Uncle Gerrit had refilled all the cups and climbed back on his stool beside the stove. Then he began to explain the purpose of the meeting.

The gist of what he said was that although the invasion seemed to be going quite slowly, as a matter of fact, it was going better than expected. Huge amounts of troops and supplies were landing in Normandy, and it wouldn't be long before the Allies would hit the German lines with tremendous force. Then it would be only days or weeks before the liberation army reached Drenthe. When that happened, the resistance in this area had to be ready to form a guerilla force behind the German front to harass the enemy. Just before that time, the resistance fighters would probably be issued uniforms and certainly weapons, which would be dropped in some isolated spot by a plane. It would be a good idea to be on the lookout for a suitable spot from now on.

"I see all your eyes lighting up," said Vander May, "and I know you all hope that day isn't far off! I do too. But, remember, I'm telling you this in the strictest confidence. You'll be tempted to spread the good news around to your friends and family, but bite your tongues, boys! What we're plotting here is no birthday party. It's dangerous! A slip of the tongue could cost us lives. You will be taking a huge responsibility upon yourselves, toward each other, and toward the rest of the nation. Anyone who is not sure that he wants in, now is the time to say so. You can still pull out!"

Vander May paused. Silence. No one even moved. They all had their eyes fixed on their leader.

"We'll have to take measures to safeguard ourselves, of course," said Vander May. "We've got to be extremely careful! From now on we will meet here every Saturday night. Saturday evenings and Sunday mornings, we run the least chance of being stopped on the road for a spot check, because that's when the National Guard usually takes some time off. If we have to meet earlier in the week, Uncle Gerrit will inform you. So he has to have your addresses, but there's no need to give your address to others in the group.

"Don't ask too many questions of one another about family or friends. Don't undertake risky adventures on your own; the group needs you. And let me repeat it! Don't discuss this work anywhere, anytime, with anybody! Not with your mother, your sister, or your girlfriend. Not even with your dog! Say nothing when things are going well, and say nothing when things go badly. Also, say nothing if you're taken prisoner. Try to give us at least forty-eight hours if you can. More we won't demand from you, because we all know the tortures used by the Germans to extract information from prisoners. Forty-eight hours is enough to allow the rest of us to get away. Understood?"

Everyone mumbled and nodded.

"I don't want to sound melodramatic, but I'd like to get a promise from each of you individually," said Vander May. "Everyone join hands. Uncle Gerrit, you too." They formed a circle, Uncle Gerrit coming to stand between Fritz and John.

"Respond when I say your name," said Vander May. "In the name of the Queen, I ask you to swear that you'll remain true to everything decided here tonight. I so swear. And you, Fritz?"

"Yes, I swear," said Fritz.

"John?"

"Yes," said John without hesitation. His doubt was gone. He couldn't pull out of the struggle now that the end was in sight.

"Steve?"

"Yes!" Steve's answer rang out solid and sure.

Then followed George, Jack, Arend, and last of all, Uncle Gerrit.

"Yes," he said, "and God bless you and your work, fellows. Remember, we're fighting for truth and justice, so we may look to Him for help."

He held up his old gnarled hands as if he were blessing the whole circle. He stood there like a guardian angel or a priest, and they were all struck by the solemnity of the moment.

"I'll never forget this picture," thought John. "Good old Uncle Gerrit! May he be spared to see the end that he predicted long ago on the first day of the war."

Everyone's throat was parched after the ceremony, and Uncle Gerrit once more made the rounds with his inexhaustible coffee pot and put a platter of sandwiches in the middle of the table, as the meeting continued.

"For the time being, it's wait and see," said Vander May, "but we're not just going to sit still while we're waiting. Sometimes we'll take a hand here and there to protect the people from the Germans. I have a couple of jobs I'd like to put before the group now, and I want to hear your reactions. First, should we send a warning to some of the more fanatical members of the N.S.M.? You all know the situation they're in. They can see that the war is lost for their German allies. So some of them are pulling in their horns. I know a National Guardsman, for example, who has turned in his rifle and cut all his ties with the N.S.M.

"But there are others who are becoming more vicious than ever. They're full of hate, and, count on it, some of those fanatics will resist to the end. But suppose we drew up a friendly little letter and sent it to their homes? Maybe that would make some of them stop and think."

"Not a bad idea," said Uncle Gerrit. "It certainly can't do any harm to try. We might also post a few letters around places where they hang out. Like on the door of their local headquarters."

The group decided that Vander May should compose the letter with the help of Uncle Gerrit. Vander May knew a place where he could get the letters stenciled. If they were finished, he would bring them along to the next meeting.

"Another thing," said Vander May. "Every day the

Germans are putting hundreds of Dutchmen to work all over the province building fortifications for them. There's no way we can stop the work, of course, but when the Allies come, they should be told where those defenses are. So we should be drawing maps marking the location of all such things as antitank trenches and pillboxes. But how are we going to get that kind of information? Any ideas?"

"My father and I have received notices to report for work on German fortifications," said Jack. "We're supposed to report to Smildervaart on Monday morning."

"And what does your father plan to do?"

"Oh, he's set on refusing, of course. If necessary, he's ready to go into hiding with the whole family."

"Either of you done any drawing?"

"My father's a carpenter and a contractor, so he's worked with blueprints. And I've had some drafting at technical school."

"You two have an ideal opportunity. Talk your father into reporting with you, presumably to work, but in reality . . . well, you know. Would your father be willing, do you think?"

"I'm sure he would, except that he's been telling everyone else *not* to report. He'll look like a traitor!" said Jack.

"Yeah, that's too bad," said Vander May. "And you can't tell anyone why he changed his mind. But you talk to him, Jack, and tell him how important this is."

"I know somebody in Assen who, I'm sure, would be willing to do the same thing," said Fritz. "He's already working on the German fortifications. He didn't dare refuse because he's hiding Jewish divers, but he hates helping the Germans!"

"Great! You take care of it, Fritz. I think someone else may already be covering that area, but two maps are better than none. Anything else?"

"Yes," said George, "we've got a touchy situation in my home town. Twice in the last few weeks our local postmaster, a reliable man, has come across letters addressed to S.D. headquarters in Assen. Instead of mailing them, he opened them; they were both anonymous letters written by the same hand. The first letter reported a local farmer for harboring divers and the next one claimed that another farmer had illegally butchered a cow. The latter wasn't even true! Sure, the man had butchered, but only for personal use.

"First, the postmaster couldn't figure out who it could be, but he saved the letters, and one day he came across a letter with the same handwriting which carried a return address. The letter-writer is an old bachelor, the local tailor, who lives all by himself. The last letter was just an order for material. A few days later the man came to the post office to buy stamps. In order to make sure he wasn't mistaken about matching the handwriting, the postmaster marked each of the stamps with a little red dot. And, sure enough, a few days later there was another anonymous letter addressed to the S.D. and it carried one of the marked stamps. What do you do with a man like that?"

"Shoot him," Steve said calmly.

"Hey, wait a minute. Not so fast," said Uncle Gerrit. "He's a human being!"

"No he isn't. He's a dirty dog, a traitor!"

"Why do you think he does it?" asked Vander May. "Is he a Nazi?"

"No, everyone seems to think he's loyal. That's how come he gets to know so much. Want to know what I think? He's a small, deformed man who has been made the butt of all kinds of jokes—some of them mean—not just by kids, but even by some adults. Whenever he gets angry, he spits and rants and carries on so outrageously that everyone thinks it's funny. I think he's bitter. He probably hates everybody, and this is his way of getting even."

"Poor man," said Uncle Gerrit. "But he's also very dangerous."

"That's exactly what our postmaster said."

"But I know a way to cure him," said Vander May. "We'll make him hate the Germans more than his neighbors."

"How are you going to do that?"

"Suppose a couple of us, dressed as Germans, paid him a visit. I'm the German: 'Listen, you little runt, you think we've got nothing better to do than follow up crank letters written by pitiful wretches who've got nothing else to do? If you bother us again, we'll walk you through town in your underwear.' And so on. Really lay it on! Slap him around a little and bust up a little of his furniture. Something he'll remember for a long time. Well, boys? Any volunteers? We've got the uniforms already. How about you, Steve? John could go with you."

"But I don't speak a word of German," objected Steve.

"No matter. You let John do all the talking, and you can handle the rough stuff. Or did you have other plans for the next couple of days, John?"

"Yeah, I really did. You know, Josh, I, well, I . . . ."

Fritz started to laugh. "Come on, John! Go along," he

urged. "Then you'll make Tricia a prophet."

"What do you mean?"

"She's the one who got us the uniforms. When she was bringing them here on the back of her bike, she was stopped by the National Guard. 'What's in the suitcase?' one of them asked. 'Clothes,' she said. And when the guy ordered her to open it, guess what your clever little sister said then? 'Don't mess it up,' she said, 'because it belongs to my brother. He's in the S.S. and he's home on leave right now. I'm just bringing his uniform back from the cleaners.' And then she leaned forward, fixed her big blue eyes on the man, and added in an awed voice, 'There were blood stains in it from the Russian front.' Man, those guys almost jumped to attention and . . . . Ouch! Uncle Gerrit, stop it. That hurts!"

"You blockhead!" fumed Uncle Gerrit. "If only your brain was as fast as your mouth!"

George roared with laughter. "Don't worry, you haven't given away much," he said. "It took me about two minutes to figure out you two were brothers. Anyone seeing you side by side can see you're chips off the same block. Ha, ha! Fritzie boy, did you ever slip up! There, there, don't look so sad, Fritzie. Uncle Gerrit didn't mean to hurt you. Give him another cookie, Uncle Gerrit."

"It was a dumb idea, anyway," grumbled Fritz, shamefaced. "When you're among strangers, sure, you have to watch what you're saying. But here we're among friends. Why should we have secrets from one another?"

"Secrets?" asked Steve. "What secrets? Tell me, what . . . ?"

"But I thought your brother was . . . ," Jack started to say.

"Not now, boys," interrupted Vander May. "You can discuss that later. Let's finish our business first. Steve, I'll go with you to visit that tailor. I'll let you know when. Any other business? Steve, I believe you had something?"

Steve was from an isolated village that cars could reach only by the road that passed right in front of Uncle Gerrit's house. The village was a haven for many divers, so a warning system had been rigged up to let the villagers know when suspicious-looking visitors were headed their way. Along the road just outside the village stood a huge windmill with one damaged arm. When the windmill was stopped with its damaged arm pointing to the sky, everyone knew that visitors were coming. But recently a car with two National Guardsmen had arrived in the middle of the village before anyone noticed that the windmill arms were in the warning position. So the villagers needed earlier warning. Was there anybody hereabouts who had a telephone and could be trusted to call the miller? The miller had been given a phone because he was considered important for food production. With the shortage of power, windmills were indispensable for grinding wheat.

Uncle Gerrit had an idea. He knew a N.S.M. member nearby who was actually in league with the underground. He still had a phone because he belonged to the party. Moreover, there was always someone home at his place because he was hiding two Jews.

"Garth Reinders!" thought John.

"The two divers can take turns watching the road," suggested Uncle Gerrit. "But we need a code. How about this: if, say, four Germans or National Guardsmen came by, the divers would call up and say, 'I'm delivering four sacks of coal.' You got that, Steve? Make sure you tell the miller."

Time passed quickly as these and other matters were discussed and plans made. Soon they were all yawning, and Steve's eyelids kept dropping shut. Uncle Gerrit's old clock creaked and then chimed three times.

Suddenly they were all on their feet as the loud clatter of falling milk cans shattered the quiet of the night, and then footsteps stomped alongside the house.

"John, George, take the back door!" hissed Vander May, pulling out his pistol. He spoke softly, but his voice was hard as steel. "Over here, Fritz, at the side door. Uncle Gerrit, douse the light! Any other way of getting in? Through the shed? Okay, you take that route, Steve! Remember, no shooting unless it's necessary."

They waited, their hearts pounding in their throats. Outside, everything was quiet. Faint light filtered into the room through the cracks around the blackout curtains. Something creaked—the door to the shed?

"Steve?" whispered Vander May.

No response.

But now they heard footsteps moving around the house again. Then more footsteps were clumping beside the house, and a loud thump on the side door made it rattle on its hinges.

Suddenly, loud laughter from outside.

Uncle Gerrit yanked open the side door. There, chewing on a mouthful of grass, stood Uncle Gerrit's cow. Behind her stood Steve, doubled up with laughter. He had sneaked out through the shed door to jump the intruder from

behind. The cow had broken out of the pasture and headed for home.

"Hands up!" roared Steve, pointing at all their gaping faces.

It had been a long, strenuous night, and the scare had undermined everyone's self-control. They all burst into laughter and laughed till their bellies ached and their legs went limp. Even Uncle Gerrit and Vander May had tears coursing down their cheeks.

The fresh morning breeze with its smell of hay and flowers came in through the open door and revitalized them all. Uncle Gerrit tied up his cow again and collected his posts and milk cans while the others played around by the pump, splashing water over their heads to waken themselves for the trip home. One by one they got their bicycles ready, said goodbye, and pedaled down the path into the dissolving dusk. It was about four o'clock in the morning. Curfew was over.

When the sun climbed over the horizon, John, Fritz, Uncle Gerrit, and Josh Vander May sat down on the wooden bench on the east side of the house to bask themselves in its warm rays. There, John told the story of his escape. As he described his trip home, he remembered the briefcase that he had picked up in the train, and he hurried to fetch it out of his suitcase. Together they read through the S.D. documents. The transcripts were only two days old. One man had confessed to hiding English pilots and had given the names of the persons who had brought them as well as of the man he had delivered them to. The first lived near the city of Groningen and the latter in a small town in Friesland.

"We've got to warn them both today," said Vander May. "The first one owns a business, so he probably has a phone. I'll take care of him. Fritz, you'll have to warn the other man in person. Be careful! The place may be staked out already. Let the air out of one of your tires and ask to borrow a bicycle pump."

Fritz sighed. "I was looking forward to a peaceful day with John. Oh, well, the work must go on. If you'll fix me a couple of sandwiches, Uncle Gerrit, I'll check out my bike and get ready to go. What's the name of that town again? Why, that's not far from where Rita's staying."

"Should I go?" John suggested eagerly.

"Listen to him! Now all of a sudden he wants to go. Hey, why don't we *both* go? It would be fun!"

"No, John. Don't do it," advised Uncle Gerrit. "At his age Fritz doesn't arouse suspicion. Tell you what, Fritz, ask her to come down for a couple of days. Even if you went, John, she's working in a big hospital, and she might be on duty. That's no place for a reunion. Fritz, tie a fishing pole to your bike; then no one will give you a second look. Shouldn't you sleep a couple of hours first? It's a long trip."

"I wouldn't be able to sleep anyway, knowing that a loyal citizen might be picked up in the meantime."

"You're a good man, Fritz," said John.

"Thanks, but that doesn't get me my sandwiches," he replied with a grin. "And I can't trade in a compliment for ration cards."

Nevertheless, he blushed with pleasure at the praise from his big brother. He punched John and blocked his jab. Then they were rolling in the grass, and Fritz ended up on top. John was still panting when Fritz rode away laughing and waving.

"It's been a long time since I've seen him so happy," said Uncle Gerrit, watching him go.

CHAPTER FOUR

After Vander May left, John and Uncle Gerrit sat and talked until John began nodding off. Uncle Gerrit offered John his bed, but John preferred to climb up into the haystack. When he awoke a few hours later to the crowing of a rooster, he had one thought on his mind: to see Mother.

He was looking over the old bicycle lent him by the blacksmith when Uncle Gerrit came outside.

"Have you got anything to fix a flat?" asked John.

"What's your hurry?" said Uncle Gerrit. "First, I've got a little job I want you to help me with. Then I'll help you."

"Yes, but . . . ."

"If you don't help *me*, I won't help *you*!"

John followed Uncle Gerrit into the field behind the house to where a big pile of peat blocks were stacked up for winter fuel. Uncle Gerrit looked around in all directions. There was no one to be seen.

"I know it's Sunday, but if you want to see your mother,

you'll have to help me put a dent in that pile," said Uncle Gerrit. "I'll leave the biggest ones for you."

In a couple minutes, John's fingers scraped something hard. When he lifted away the next peat block, he saw the seat of a bike. Soon he was looking at a beautiful bicycle, complete with excellent tires.

"Uncle Gerrit! Where on earth did you latch onto such a prize!"

"Look at that," said Uncle Gerrit. "Not a spot of rust anywhere. Not even on the handlebars. There's not a better place in the world to stash a bike. The peat soaks up all the moisture. Where did I get it? Where does a dog get fleas? Here, help me fix the pile the way it was."

As they walked back to the house, John got the whole story.

"This is the first time in my life I ever stole anything," said Uncle Gerrit. "Or would you call it spoils of war? I'm not sure myself. It happened in February, the day after we heard that you had been picked up. I had spent kind of a rough night, and in the morning I got claustrophobia; I had to get out for a while. I was sure that your father would come back, but I didn't want to lose you either.

"I went for a walk across the fields trying to get some peace of mind. And I sat down on a stump to catch my breath. That's when I got my vision—I don't know what else to call it—of you and Fritz coming up the path together, just like you did last night. It was as real and lifelike as you are right now! I thanked God for it, and when I walked home, I felt twenty years younger.

"When I came to the canal, there were a half dozen National Guardsmen out hunting rabbits. In February, mind you, right after they had littered. All the other hunters had long since turned in their rifles, of course, but these guys were having a wild old time, popping away at anything that hopped. They had parked their bikes against a couple of trees along the canal. I stood and watched a while, and you know how it is, whenever I'm thankful or happy, I begin to think like a boy again—not a very good boy, I'm afraid. I was a brassy little devil when I was young.

"I said to myself, 'You guys have your fun, and I'll have mine.' So I picked out the best-looking bike of the lot and, sploosh, into the canal it went! And believe it or not, I already had you in mind. A couple days later I came back after sunset and fished it out. A little grease and a new coat of paint, and it looked like new. Even the owner wouldn't recognize it. So there you are! Put a little air in the tires and enjoy it. Only, we've got to get you a good permit; otherwise, the Germans will grab it the first time they stop you. We'll have to talk to Josh about that next time."

"Uncle Gerrit, you're the greatest! If we didn't have you . . . ."

Uncle Gerrit nodded emphatically. "Right, right! If you didn't have me and two good eyes, you'd be blind as a bat. Go on, you chucklehead, fix yourself a sandwich and go make your mother happy. But first give me that thing that's making the bulge in your pants pocket. That can only bring you trouble."

It was almost afternoon by the time John approached Mother's latest place of residence. The farmer's name was Niemeyer, John knew, but he thought it best to find the place without asking any questions. It had to be somewhere in this neighborhood. He cycled along very slowly, studying the houses. Turning a corner, he met two children strolling down the street, hand in hand—his sister Hanneke and little Hansie! His heart leaped as he recognized them.

Quickly he stopped and pretended that the chain had come off his bike. When he looked up, his little sister's eyes were riveted on him. He smiled at her, and she turned fiery red and warily looked about as she drew closer. Hansie acted shy. He didn't recognize John any longer. Hanneke stopped at a distance of several feet.

"John!" she said. "Oh, John!"

John straightened up and took a step toward her.

But she moved back and said, "No, John! Ride on! The people across the road are dangerous."

He followed her glance to the house beside the road, where two curious faces were all but pressed against the window. He was amazed at how well his baby sister had her wits about her.

"Which house is yours?" John asked.

"The third one on the right, with the thatched roof. Oh, John, Mom will be so happy to see you!"

"You come home right away too, okay? I want to give you a great big hug."

She smiled and nodded and, as a woman cycled by, she said loudly, "You're welcome, sir."

John hopped back on his bike and counted three farmhouses and turned onto a neat farmyard. As he neared the house, he saw a shape flitting past the window and immediately recognized his mother. On the door of the house was a large sign: SCARLET FEVER. He forgot about it until he had embraced Mother for the third time and was wiping the tears from his eyes.

"Does Trudy have scarlet fever, Mom?" he asked anxiously.

"No, don't worry. She just has a touch of German measles," said Mother. "The doctor gave us that sign to keep the Germans away. Lately, they've been making quite a few house searches in this area. The Germans are deathly scared of contagious diseases, however, so now we're pretty safe. Quick, come inside! Oh, I couldn't believe my eyes when I saw you coming up the drive!"

She stopped a moment at the door. "You can tell me everything in front of these people," she whispered. "They're fabulous people! We need have no secrets from them."

Mr. and Mrs. Niemeyer did seem to be a very fine old couple. They were as happy to see John as if he had been their own son coming home. But John didn't tell everything. He couldn't. He looked at Mother and saw how terribly she had aged; the anxious months were etched into her face. She had worries enough without knowing that he had escaped death by only a single step. He pretended that he had simply been released, and he related only the good times that he had experienced in prison.

Besides, he didn't get much of a chance to tell his story, for suddenly Hanneke came rushing into the room and threw her arms about his neck, sobbing. Hansie also climbed up on his knee. Although he probably didn't actually recognize John, he did sense something special and familiar about him. A few minutes later the living room door squeaked open and in came Trudy in her pajamas.

She had heard that something was going on downstairs. So another joyful reunion followed.

The two girls immediately understood when Mother warned them to tell no one that their brother had been here. They were to call him John De Jong and say that he worked for a baker in Assen.

That afternoon when John and Mother were alone, she told him all that she knew about Father. Six months ago, she had received a letter from him which had been smuggled out of a camp somewhere near Wolfenbüttel; at least, that was where it had been stamped. She dug the letter out of her purse and gave it to John to read. It was very carefully phrased, for all letters leaving Germany were subject to censorship. Father wrote as if he were a volunteer working in a German factory. "I'm doing very well," he wrote. "Don't worry about me, although I may not get any leave before the end of the war." In a postscript, he added: "Send my greetings and blessings to John, and tell him to be careful about his health."

The message was quite clear to John: Don't risk your life; you must survive.

Mother had more news. A little over a month ago, a young man, a resistance worker had paid her a visit. He told her that he had escaped from a camp near Hamburg, where he had met Father and they had become good friends. While he was part of a work gang that worked outside the fence, he had seen a chance to escape. The only person he had taken into his confidence was Father, who had encouraged him and supplied him with extra rations, a good map of Germany, and regular clothes.

"I never would have made it without him," the young

man told her. "Your husband is standing up magnificently against the Germans, Mrs. De Boer. He's an inspiration to all the other prisoners. They'll never crush him! I'm sure you'll see him again, someday soon."

But then he told her such depressing stories about the heavy labor in the camp and the beatings and especially the hunger suffered by the men that he almost destroyed the impact of his earlier words.

"Now that we know where he is," said Mother, "we send him two parcels of food a week. Uncle Gerrit and some other friends are also sending him food parcels. Do you think he gets them, John? When I lie awake at night, I see him before me starved and weak. And then I think of you, and of Fritz, who has stopped going to school altogether, and of Tricia, who is also involved in goodness knows what, and then sometimes I can't take any more. During the day, every time someone comes onto the yard, my heart nearly stops because I'm afraid he's come to tell me something has happened to one of you.

"But now God has given you back to me, John. Please promise me that from now on you'll take it easy and keep out of resistance work. Honestly, I can't stand it any more to live in fear for all of you night and day. The Allies are winning without you, aren't they? You've done enough!"

It wasn't like Mother to give in to such anxiety. Her perpetual worrying about Father and her oldest children had drained her of all courage.

"You spend too much time fretting about us, Mom," said John. "You should get out once in a while. Why don't you go and visit Aunt Haddie for a few days? Or, I know what, maybe we can find you a house somewhere near Uncle Gerrit's place. Then you'll be back in our old neighborhood. You really don't have to worry about me any longer. I won't let myself be caught a second time. I'll be careful. Nor should you be afraid for Father. That man was right. Father can look after himself. He'll make it. That's what Uncle Gerrit says too, and he has known Father since birth. What good does it do to worry yourself to a frazzle?"

And then he told her about his talk with Mrs. Versteeg, the wife of the farmer with whom he had stayed after his escape. He quoted the text that had meant so much to him then: "Cast all your cares on Him." He was delighted to see a smile come to her lips. Putting his arms around her, he said happily, "You'll see, Mom, in a little while the war will be over, and you know what we'll do then? We'll take a car to Germany and go pick up Father. We won't leave him there a day longer than necessary. What do you say about that?"

He said it just to cheer her up, but when the words were out, he thought, "Why not? Who knows? Maybe that day isn't so far off." The idea kept returning to his mind all day long, and he resolved to keep an eye out for a good car.

In the afternoon, Mr. and Mrs. Niemeyer went to church. Mother stayed home to visit with John, of course. He couldn't go to church, for several people in the congregation knew him. He was playing a game with Hanneke and Trudy and Hansie, when he heard bicycles on the yard. It was Fritz with two girls—Tricia and Rita! John went tearing outside. The little farmhouse was almost too small to hold so much joy!

Mother had all her children with her once again, and they

had a Sunday evening like they hadn't had for many, many months. As the light faded, they had to sit by the dim light of a kerosene lamp because their ration of electricity had already been used up. The evening became a full-fledged celebration when Tricia told them that she had passed her finals with honors. So she had graduated ahead of her older brother.

"I bet you'll be able to take your exams next year, John," she said. "Why don't you start reviewing now? You can use my books."

Mother leaped at the suggestion. "Do that, John! Now that you're staying with Uncle Gerrit, where it's nice and quiet, you should have all kinds of time to do some studying."

"What?" said Fritz, looking up in surprise.

But John nudged him under the table and, just to set her mind at rest, he promised Mother that he would try to get back to the books.

Tricia and Rita had to leave before eleven to get to the teacher's house where Tricia was living. Rita had been invited to stay with her. Fritz had to return to the baker's house. Rita was back early the next morning, however, for she had taken two days off from the hospital. She had been forced to leave Rotterdam about two months ago because the Germans had found out about her role in hiding Jews. They had come to the hospital to arrest her, but a doctor had quickly tucked her into bed on the ward where she was working and swaddled her head with bandages. When the Germans came on the ward, she lay in bed moaning, and they hadn't suspected a thing.

The next day John visited the baker who had taken in

Fritz. The man gave him a white jacket and a basket used by his delivery boys. When Rita's stay was over, John escorted her back to the hospital dressed as a baker's helper, and from there he returned to Uncle Gerrit's house. On the way back, he was stopped twice by Germans and National Guardsmen, but they were completely fooled by his disguise. The second time he was frisked, so he was thankful that Uncle Gerrit had kept his revolver.

When he returned, Uncle Gerrit told him that he had found him a good place to stay. He would be staying at the home of Garth Reinders, an old friend of Father's who was a member of the N.S.M. but who actually reported all their doings to the underground. No one would think of searching his house. John was given a little room in the attic with a small window overlooking the road. Tricia brought him her books, but he leafed through them once and then stacked them in a corner. He knew that he wouldn't get much studying done until the war was over.

Uncle Gerrit had repaired the blacksmith's bike that John had borrowed, and one drizzly afternoon John took it back as he had promised. Mr. Havinga, the blacksmith, was very happy to see him, for he had a problem.

"That Mr. Vos you brought here," he said. "What a strange one! I kind of took to him at first, but not for long. Are you sure that guy can be trusted? He talks too much! And that's not all. The man who fixed his I.D. is an official at the local distribution office, and when he brought over the new I.D., he also gave Vos a ration card. Vos offered the official ten guilders apiece for them. When the man got angry, this Vos pretended he was only testing him, and he started laying it on like he's one of the bigshots in the underground. By then I knew better. Later, he offered to sell us guns, if we met his price. He told us you bought one from him and that you paid him one hundred guilders. He even showed us a receipt."

"Why, that liar!" John exclaimed angrily. "You're right, he's not to be trusted. I guess I didn't feel entirely right about him, but I didn't think . . . ."

"You should have tipped us off if you had any suspicions," said the blacksmith, shaking his head. "Now he's our headache. He could betray us all!" John agreed that he had been too gullible.

"Leave me an address where I can reach you," said Havinga. "If he shows up again, we'll let you know. Then you see to it that he doesn't cause us any trouble. I don't care how."

John gave him Garth Reinders' phone number and told the smith that he would come immediately in response to the message: "Havinga says your bike is fixed."

"I've got a little treat in store for our jolly comedian," said John angrily. "But maybe I can find out where he lives. I know he's from the city of Groningen."

"I can help you there," said Havinga. "I've got his complete address. He asked for an I.D. with his own name and address. All he wanted changed was his age."

"Then there's no problem," John assured the blacksmith. "Don't worry, Havinga; I'll make sure our mutual friend stays in line. Leave him to me!"

That Saturday evening when the group met at Uncle Gerrit's house, John told them the story. Vander May took it quite seriously.

"He must be a black marketeer," he said. "Most of

those creeps have no conscience. Anything to make a quick buck. This guy sounds like one of the worst, judging from his proposal to sell guns to the underground. We've got to keep a close eye on him. When Havinga gives you a call, let me know. I'd like to go with you."

He and Fritz had several friends in Groningen whom they could count on. Because it was easier for Fritz to move around, he was appointed to look into Mr. Vos's operations.

The squad meeting was just as convivial as the week before. Jack showed them a couple of beautifully drawn maps clearly marking the location of the German fortifications being built in their district. Fritz told them that similar maps were being made of the area around Assen. Vander May had a hundred duplicated copies of the letter that he and Uncle Gerrit had drawn up to members of the N.S.M. He had also managed to get a list of known party members in the area and their addresses. John would prepare the envelopes, and Fritz would mail them when he was in Groningen. "Remember, John, type the addresses."

Fritz had devised an ingenious way to transport such items. He tucked them away inside an old accordion that he hung over his shoulder by a strap. It had already proven its worth several times, for Fritz had been stopped while carrying it on three occasions, and no one had ever thought to ask about the accordion.

In his laconic way, Steve reported on the visit he and Vander May had made to the letter-writing tailor in George's home town. They had put such a scare into the little man that he had crawled underneath his workbench and begged for mercy as Steve and Vander May threatened him and smashed some of his furniture.

"And now, if you please, don't ever send me on such a job again," he said morosely. "I'd rather trade punches with an entire patrol of German troops."

But George told them that the tailor had become the hero of the village overnight. Everyone in town felt sorry for the man because of his ill treatment at the hands of the Germans, and many people had come to offer him help, some carrying gifts to replace things that had been broken during the raid.

"Beautiful!" said Vander May. "Heaping coals upon his head. That might even cure him."

Nothing special happened during the next few weeks, and John settled into a peaceful routine. He began studying for his exams and found himself enjoying it. Occasionally, he did small jobs for Uncle Gerrit or Vander May. One day he was asked to pick up a professor from the train and escort him to a big farm. The farmer was hiding several university students, and the professor spent a solid week at the farm lecturing to them on history. When John took the professor back to the station a week later, his suitcase was heavy with meat and cheese. Periodically, John also distributed ration cards to homes where divers were hiding.

He also made another trip to see Havinga, the blacksmith, and to tell him that Vos was under close observation by the underground in Groningen. In his investigation, Fritz had discovered that the man was indeed a black market dealer, but the local underground had always considered him a sort of harmless rascal. Now they were taking another look at him. Keeping a close eye on him wasn't very difficult, because his neighbor was a loyal resistance man.

That night John stayed at the Job Eising farm so that he could roam about the area early the next morning and sketch the lay of the land. It had occurred to him that this isolated area would be an ideal spot for an air drop when it came time for the Allies to deliver their weapons. No N.S.M. members were known to live in the area, and the tract of land that John had in mind had no real roads leading to it—only a few narrow trails.

When Vander May saw the map, he went to reconnoiter the area himself and came back very pleased with John's find. He forwarded a description of the terrain to an address known only to him; from there it would be transmitted to England by radio. The code sentence agreed on was, "John has made a good catch." When the English were ready, it would be broadcast at night on Radio Orange right after the news. They couldn't pinpoint the time or date exactly, but the drop would come on one of the nights immediately following the transmission of the code words.

The whole group hoped that it would be soon, for the war news was becoming more encouraging every day. On the eastern front, the Russians had the Germans on the run and were quickly approaching the border of Poland. The Allies had taken almost all of Normandy. A Dutch unit was also fighting in France—the Princess Irene Brigade. It was composed of Dutchmen who had fled across the Channel.

Then one night came the electrifying news of an attempt on Hitler's life. The announcement came over one of the Nazi-controlled stations. While Hitler was conducting talks with Mussolini at Hitler's headquarters, said the announcer, a bomb had exploded in the building. Although several high-ranking officers had been killed, Hitler had received only a minor wound. The announcer spoke of it as a miracle wrought by providence that the Feuhrer had been spared. But most people whispered that he had made a pact with the devil.

Nevertheless, it did raise hopes that the war might be over one of these days. The bombing attempt showed that there was strong opposition to Hitler within Germany. Nothing further happened, however. Rumors did leak out about a brutal, bloody purge among German officialdom. The beloved Fuehrer was raging through his own staff like an avenging fury. At the same time, the occupation troops in Holland became increasingly severe. Curfew was moved up to ten o'clock, and anyone caught out after that time had a good chance of being shot. Some National Guardsmen prowled the streets like rabid dogs, ready to sink their teeth into any vulnerable person. But others saw the coming liberation, and were looking for ways to pacify the oppressed people.

Arend told about his father's neighbor who had been an enthusiastic N.S.M. member since the beginning of the war. One day he squeezed through the hedge to have a little chat. As he was about to go, he said, "Listen, I thought I'd better warn you about the divers you're hiding."

"Divers? What divers?" sputtered Arend's father.

"No need to worry. I won't give you away," said the neighbor, "but there's been talk, and one of these days the National Guard is going to surprise you with a house search. But if it happens, I'll be with them, and I'll see to it that I'm posted at the back door. So when the others are banging on the front door, send your divers out through the back. They can jump over the fence and hide in my haystack. Nobody'll look for them there. By the way, you won't forget that I helped you, will you?"

Less than a week later, it happened just as the man had said. The National Guard raided the farmhouse in the middle of the night. By the time they were inside, Arend had led the divers across the back yard and into the neighbor's haystack, so the Nazis found nothing.

"But I'm not sure he wasn't the one who suggested the raid in the first place so that he would come out smelling like a rose," said Arend. "But I guess we can look into that after the war."

As Arend told his story, they were all sitting around waiting for Fritz to show up for their regular Saturday meeting. Fritz had never been late before, so the group was getting more and more uneasy as time passed.

"Does anybody know what he's been doing today?" asked Vander May.

"I met him yesterday at Mother's," said John. "He was going to escort Tricia to Groningen. I don't know exactly what they were doing, but I think that they were delivering a message for our friends in Assen."

"I'm afraid something has happened," said Vander May.

Just then they heard a bicycle bell ringing outside and voices. No, it wasn't Fritz's voice. It sounded like a girl. Jack was leading her down the path to the house. It was Tricia! As she entered the room, it was obvious that she had bad news.

"This lady says she has business here and that she's here on behalf of Fritz," Jack reported. "But she doesn't know the password."

"She's okay!" John and Vander May cried simultaneously. "What's the matter, Trish? Where's Fritz?"

"The National Guard's got him," said Tricia, biting her lip.

"You mean they arrested him?"

"No, he went with them voluntarily. But I bet they've locked him up by now."

"How come? Whereabouts?"

Tricia mentioned the name of a small town on the way to Groningen. John jumped up. "What say, Josh? Let's all go and break him out of there right now!"

"Wait a minute!" said Vander May. "Of course we'll help him, but first we've got to know a little more. Let's hear everything that happened, Tricia."

Uncle Gerrit handed her a glass of water, which she gulped down thirstily.

"Oh, he was in a crazy mood all day," she said. "In Groningen he purposely bumped into a German officer who was just coming out of a liquor store with two bottles of wine. The bottles smashed on the sidewalk and the man was furious. I think he was about ready to drag Fritz off to jail.

"Later, we went into a café for a cup of coffee. At first I didn't want to go in because the place was full of Krauts, but Fritz insisted. I think he got a charge out of it. Just as we were getting ready to leave, a German officer came in with a lady, and I said, 'Oh, look what a pretty shawl she's wearing!' Right away I wished I'd kept my mouth shut, because Fritz cried, 'Would you like to have it?' I begged him not to do anything foolish, but he insisted that the German had probably stolen it for her. Finally, he said, 'Okay, forget it.' He paid for our coffee, and we went outside. But at the door, he turned around and said, 'Wait a minute. I've got to go to the bathroom a minute.'

"As he came out of the bathroom, he walked past the coatrack, and when he got outside, he handed me the shawl. See? This is it."

George laughed in admiration, and the others joined in. But Vander May looked angry, and John prodded Tricia. "Well, what happened then. Did the guy come after Fritz, or what?"

"No, nobody saw him."

"Then why was he picked up? Come on, Trish! We're wasting time!"

"Well, when we were on the way home, we were stopped by a Guardsman, a young guy who was all by himself. He asked us for our I.D.'s. I showed mine, but Fritz refused to show his. 'First you show me *your* papers,' Fritz said. 'Anybody can say he belongs to the National Guard. How do I know you're not an imposter?'

"I don't know if the man didn't have his papers with him, or if he was just acting stubborn like Fritz, but he refused to let Fritz go. 'You're coming along to see the commandant,' he said. 'That's fine with me,' said Fritz. 'It's on my way home anyway.'

"And then the two of us followed the fellow into the next town, Fritz carrying his accordion."

"Did he have anything inside his accordion?" asked Vander May.

"Just a handful of leaflets that had been tossed from an airplane somewhere along the road. *The Flying Dutchman*, I think it was called. And his gun! He had his gun in there too. I just don't understand what he was up to. When he got to the headquarters of the National Guard, he told me to wait outside. 'I'll be out in a minute,' he said. Well, I waited for fifteen minutes, and then Fritz came to the window and motioned to me to go on without him. He was smiling, but I bet he isn't smiling anymore.

"Oh, John, what are we going to tell Mother? No, I didn't stop there. I just stopped at my place to tell them I wouldn't be home tonight, and then I pedaled straight here. You've just got to do something to help him!"

Then she burst into tears.

"Well, boys, what do we do?"

"Let's go get him!" they all shouted.

"All right, tell Jack to come in. Tricia, buck up! He isn't lost yet."

Vander May stopped. There was a noise outside. The door burst open and there, drenched with sweat and beaming like a cherub, stood Fritz.

"Hi guys!" he greeted them. "Hey, Trish! What on earth are you doing here? And what are you scowling about, Josh? I'm not that late. Besides, I couldn't help it."

"You come over here and sit down, mister!" Vander May said angrily. "Let's hear what you've been up to."

"Is this an interrogation?" said Fritz. "Then I'm clamming up for forty-eight hours, just as I promised."

"Fritz, quit your kidding around!" exclaimed John. "This is serious. Can't you see? We were worried sick about you! We were just getting ready to attack a National

Guard headquarters for you. Tricia came over here all upset because you had been picked up. Come on, tell us what happened! We know the story up to the time you were taken to their headquarters, so you can begin there."

"Shoot! You guys don't have to worry about me. I can take care of myself. Those jerks in the National Guard don't scare me. I just thought I'd show them that the time when they can push people around is over. Did I ever have fun with those muttonheads! When I got inside their headquarters, the commandant wasn't there, and they weren't about to let me go until their chief had questioned me. I sat there waiting for fifteen minutes and then decided that Tricia might as well go on without me, so I waved her on. I wished I hadn't, because a couple of minutes later the commandant arrived. Then I showed the guy at the desk my I.D., and he told me I was free to go.

" 'How come you didn't show your I.D. to the other fellow?' he asked me.

" 'Well,' I said, 'I can *see* that you men belong to the National Guard. But the other fellow didn't look like a Guardsman at all; he looked like such a decent fellow.'

"And the idiot didn't even catch on! Can you believe it? But the commandant did, and, boy, did he laugh! He was kind of a nice guy and he asked me if I'd like a cup of coffee—real coffee! Since Trish had left already, I said, 'Yes, please.' Of course, I didn't know she was on her way over here!"

"Is that all?"

"Just about. I sat and talked with those guys a little while. They asked me what I was doing with the accordion. 'Going to a wedding,' I said. Then they asked me to play something, but I told them, 'All I know is the national anthem. Would you like me to play that?' But they passed that up. Man, did they ever have good coffee! A lot better than Uncle Gerrit's."

"If I went around breaking into other people's houses and stealing their stuff, I'd probably have good coffee too," retorted Uncle Gerrit. "That was stolen property you were enjoying, bonny boy!"

"Don't look a gift horse in the mouth, I always say," said Fritz grinning. "I always wanted to have a look-see inside their headquarters. They even offered me a second cup! I was starting to feel spoiled. It was like enjoying honey from the lion's mouth.

"Pretty soon the commandant asks me, 'It's kind of nice here, isn't it?' 'Sure,' I says, 'except for one thing: that picture over your desk.' He had a big picture of Hitler on the wall, of course. 'What's wrong with it?' he asks. 'It's the wrong sex. Isn't there supposed to be a lady hanging there?' Oh boy, you should have seen his face. 'Get your blankety-blank tail out of here,' he screams. So I figured it was time to make tracks. And here I am! I pedaled as fast as I could. I'd have been here in time, except that I wasted half an hour looking all over Assen for Tricia."

"You're a blockhead! An irresponsible jackass!" exploded Vander May. "Don't you ever pull a stunt like that again!"

"Well, then give me something constructive to do!" shouted Fritz. "Some squad! All we hear is promises, promises, and we keep having these meetings, but we don't do a blasted thing! Isn't there anything we can do? This waiting is driving me nuts!"

"Nevertheless, you're just going to have to be patient for a while yet," said Vander May. "More, I can't promise you. But I'm sure it can't be much longer."

And he was right. A couple weeks later things began happening so fast and the squad had so much to do that they could hardly keep up.

CHAPTER FIVE

Halfway through August the long-expected Allied breakthrough in France finally occurred. At last the stubborn German resistance crumbled before the superior power that poured in from overseas. The Germans began a disorderly retreat over roads constantly strafed by English fighter planes.

The Allies—Americans, Englishmen and Canadians—allowed the Germans no chance to regroup. From Normandy they quickly fanned out in all directions in pursuit of the fleeing Germans. New landings took place in Southern France, and there, too, one city after another fell to the advancing American troops.

Large numbers of tanks, guns, and trucks were abandoned by the Germans. More than a half-million German soldiers were taken prisoner and twice that many were killed. Paris liberated itself, as the resistance came out into the open and, after some bloody house-to-house fighting, chased the occupying forces out of the city. A few days later, except for a few coastal towns, all of France was liberated, and the German general in charge of France committed suicide. Soon the Allied armies were crossing the Belgian border.

Everything went so fast that the news services couldn't keep up with the events. When the radio stations were still announcing that the Americans had reached Belgium, they were actually already entering Brussels; and when the announcer was describing the liberation of Brussels, the Americans had already crossed into the Netherlands in several places.

"But a short while my fellow countrymen," proclaimed the prime minister on Radio Orange, "and your suffering will be over!"

Wild rumors began circulating. In Rotterdam the story spread that Breda, a city just to the south, had already been liberated. The people of The Hague thought that the Americans had already taken Rotterdam, so they streamed out of the city to the main highway, lining the road and waving little flags to welcome their liberators.

This, of course, panicked the Germans, but especially the Dutch Nazis. With the whole country cheering the victorious Allies, they stampeded in confusion. They expected the American forces to arrive at any time, which would mean disaster for them. For many years their countrymen, whom they had betrayed, had threatened them with the Day of the Axe, when the heads of all collaborators would roll.

On the first Tuesday in September, later called "Crazy Tuesday," the traitors lost their nerve and began running. Large numbers fled northward, taking along their families and as much of their possessions as they could carry. The fear was contagious. Soon a turbulent flood of Germans and N.S.M. members crowded into trains or took automobiles and bicycles to seek safety in Germany. Some even began walking, pushing baby carriages and handcarts. As the exodus grew, people came out of their houses or stood by their windows watching in astonishment. Were they really going to be rid of the enemy so suddenly and so easily?

In response to an urgent message from Vander May, the young men of John's group assembled at Uncle Gerrit's house in high spirits. They were itching to attack the retreating Germans as the Parisian underground had done. But where were the promised weapons? Vander May had received a message that the location of the air drop had been approved and that the signal would be, "John has made a good catch." The last message that they had received was, "Stand by."

John had collected a number of flashlights for signaling their location to the plane dropping the weapons. He had also made arrangements with Job Eising to use his farm as a base of operations. But they sat glued to the radio every evening in vain, listening to Radio Orange at quarter to nine and also to the Belgian broadcast later in the evening. The news continued to be encouraging as one Allied victory after another was reported. But no code words! They still had nothing but a few revolvers, and they wouldn't stand a chance against the well-armed Germans.

Nevertheless, the squad felt that the time was ripe to strike at the demoralized enemy. Fritz said that he had been in Meppel and Hoogeveen that morning and that the

Germans there were ready to pull out. No one was patroling the roads anymore. He was sure that the members of the National Guard in that area were also packing up. Were they going to stand by and watch those Nazi turncoats get away scot-free? Hadn't the resistance pledged to see to it that the traitors would be tried in the place where they had committed their crimes?

"The sooner we're rid of them the better," said Uncle Gerrit. "If they leave now, they'll save us a lot of bother. That's what I say. What do you think, Josh?"

"Listening to Fritz talk, I'm glad we don't have our weapons yet," answered Vander May. "You guys sound as if you'd like to run out on the street and start taking potshots at every German and N.S.M. man in sight. That wouldn't do any good."

"Well, what would?" demanded Fritz. "Sitting here around the table doing nothing?"

"We've got to act in accordance with our orders," insisted Vander May. "We're not in this alone. I've attended quite a few planning sessions during the last weeks, and now we're part of a nation-wide underground army called the Inland Battleforces. We get our orders directly from the top, by wireless from England and then through a network of couriers. I'm the one who gets those orders, and it's your job to obey them without grumbling, even if it means just sitting here waiting for a month.

"But that won't be necessary; there are some things we *can* do. We can hurt the Germans by breaking their communication and supply lines so that they no longer know what's going on and can't get their supplies through. I've received orders to sabotage the telephone lines and railways. We don't have the equipment to tackle the railways yet, but we can sure cut the main telephone lines in the area. That's why I called you together. Look, I've got a map of our district. We'll cut the main cables here and here. Those are both vital links for the German communication with Groningen."

"How come we're cutting them way out there, Josh?" asked John. "Couldn't we cut them, say, here? That's much closer to home."

"Never foul your own nest," said Vander May. "We want to keep things as quiet as possible in this neighborhood; then the Germans won't look for us here. And remember, the Germans have announced that wherever sabotage occurs, the neighboring homes will be burned to the ground. So we want to avoid that as much as possible. The places I've picked are both deserted stretches of road. The nearest homes are a couple of kilometers away. Just to be sure, however, we'll warn the people on either side after we've cut the cable. Well, let's go, boys! Get your tools! If we travel before eight, we run less chance of being stopped."

Curfew had been changed to eight o'clock. After that, only Germans and National Guardsmen were allowed out on the streets.

"We should have four shovels and two axes. Can you help us there, Uncle Gerrit?"

Uncle Gerrit produced two shovels and one ax. John picked up the rest of the tools from his landlord.

"I always have to miss out on all the fun," grumbled Uncle Gerrit. "Make coffee and fix sandwiches! If only I were a few years younger! But there's no way you're going to keep me home when you start busting up trains. Man, that must be some sight to see one of those engines hopping the tracks. Just imagine the explosion if it's carrying munitions!"

Pedaling down the road with shovels over their shoulders, they looked like a group of indentured workers on their way home after working on the German defenses. Fritz was right, no one seemed to be patroling the roads anymore. They *did* meet many people with drawn, anxious faces hurrying along the road with suitcases and boxes—Dutch Nazis. Occasionally, they were passed by German military vehicles, also heading away from the front. Once Fritz couldn't resist shouting a jibe after them, but Vander May immediately silenced him.

They arrived at their destination early in the evening. Here the road passed through a long stretch of forest, and it was almost deserted. It seemed safe to stop by the side of the road for a brief consultation.

"You stay here, John. George, Steve—you two stay with him," ordered Vander May. "I'm planning to make you second-in-command, John, so this is your chance to show what you're made of."

"Me?" said John, flinching. "I wish you'd pick someone else, Josh."

"Not a chance!" said Vander May. "You've had more experience than any of the others. You're in charge here. Now listen! You can warn the people on that side ahead of time. They're loyal, trustworthy people. Just tell the man that Josh sent you, and he'll understand. Afterward, each group makes its own way home, but wait until after four in the morning, when the curfew expires. Carry out your orders as they've been given. Is that understood?"

"Got you, Josh," answered John. He felt a little queer at being named second-in-command, but the others seemed to think it quite normal. John handed the map to George and asked him to take Steve and pick out a likely-looking spot for the job that they had to do and then wait in the woods. Meanwhile, he cycled to the small farm that Josh had pointed out on the map.

When he arrived, the family was sitting at the table for supper—at least, the husband and four children were at the table. The wife, he was told, was in bed with a newborn child. The children were laughing at something that their father had said when John walked in. The message he had to deliver suddenly weighed very heavily on John.

"Could I speak to you outside for a minute?" he asked the farmer.

"Of course!" said the man, coming to the door. "What can I do for you?"

"Let's get a little farther from the house."

They walked a short way farther, and the farmer sat down on a milk can by the barn.

"I've got a message from Josh," began John.

"Josh?" asked the farmer. "I don't know any Josh."

That stopped John for a moment. But then he caught on. "No, of course not, because you don't know me. I'm afraid the message isn't very good news. Josh wanted me to tell you that we're going to cut the telephone cable between your place and the one north of you. You know what that might mean?"

The farmer stared at John, turning first red and then white. He leaned back against the barn and closed his eyes.

"Is that the thanks I get from Josh for all the help I've given him?" he moaned.

"I'm sorry, but this was the best location we could find," explained John. "I'd advise you to take your family and spend the night somewhere else."

"Pick up and leave with a three-day-old child and an ailing wife?" exploded the farmer angrily. He jumped up. "You guys are crazy! Why not someplace else? Why don't you cut the cable next to some Nazi's house?"

John took a deep breath. Vander May hadn't foreseen this. "Carry out your orders as they've been given." But now he was a villain.

"Listen," said John. "If you can point me to a better place that's just as safe, I'll be glad to cut the cable elsewhere. But otherwise . . . ."

"Sure, I know a better spot!" the farmer said eagerly. "You know where the road crosses the canal?"

"No, I don't know this area at all, and I left my map with the others."

"No matter, I'll draw you a map in a minute. Two N.S.M. men live near there—one on either side of the bridge. A couple of fanatics!"

"How do we get there? Along the road?"

"No, you can cut across the fields. I can point out approximately where the cable is buried. It was put in not so many years ago."

"Then you'll come along to point out the place?"

"Sure! The kids can look after themselves for a while."

Fifteen minutes later they had joined the others. George and Steve concurred with John's change of plans. The farmer led them through the darkening woods down a network of back trails until they reached the canal. Then they hid their bikes and crept along the water's edge toward the bridge. It was completely dark by the time they reached the cover of the bridge. They lay down behind some underbrush and smoked a cigarette behind cupped hands. A bike without inner tubes went clattering across the bridge, followed by a truck. Germans? Then there was no more traffic. It was now after curfew.

After an hour, John gave the signal to begin. George sneaked across the bridge to act as lookout on the other side. John kept an eye on the house on his side of the canal. The farmer used a hooded flashlight to search out the probable location of the cable on the bank of the canal. He began digging, and Steve joined in.

They were taking a long time, so John went back to look. Steve and the farmer had already dug two holes without success. The second one was already shoulder deep on Steve.

"Dig somewhere else," said John. "The cable isn't buried that deep."

He jumped into the hole and studied the map by the light of his flashlight. A soft whistle from the other bank made them all duck for cover. Two cyclists were approaching. The sound of their voices carried a long way on the quiet evening air.

"I'm telling you, they can't hold back the Americans much longer."

"It sure doesn't look good, does it? I figure they might hold out until this winter."

"I'm getting out before then. The underground is . . . ."

As they pedaled out of earshot, John could hear Steve

chuckling. Then he jumped up and began digging with renewed vigor in another spot pointed out by John.

"I think I've hit it!" he said a few minutes later. He chopped down hard with his shovel to show that he had struck something solid. The farmer handed him the ax.

"What if it's the electric cable?" asked the farmer.

"We'll find out soon enough," said Steve, lifting the ax over his head. But no sparks shot out as the ax bit through the insulation, so it had to be the telephone cable. It was very thick and tough, for Steve had to do quite a bit of strenuous chopping before he was through.

"Hello, hello!" Steve whispered into the break. "I can hear them hollering from both sides of the line."

Then they carefully filled in the holes that they had dug, and they replaced the sod so that no one could tell they had been there.

"Now we'll do the same thing on the other side of the canal," said John. "Except that there we'll be even more careful not to leave any traces.

The rest of the work was finished without any interruptions, and they were back at the farmer's house drinking coffee before midnight. Their host sliced up a loaf of bread and took down a big summer sausage hanging in the pantry. They talked quietly so as not to disturb his wife and baby. John knew that he had done the right thing by changing the location of the cut.

At four o'clock in the morning they said goodbye to the farmer and hopped on their bikes for the trip home. They made it back before the other group, so George and Steve climbed into a haystack near Uncle Gerrit's house to get a little sleep. John pedaled on to the Reinders farm, where he

was boarding. When he opened the shed to put his bike away, he found it full of N.S.M. families who had spent the night there. Two women were quarreling loudly about who was to blame for their troubles.

"It was *your* husband who persuaded *mine* to join the party!" one shouted at the other.

"Oh yeah? My man would have quit months ago if your man hadn't insisted that they stick it out!"

"Please, ladies," pleaded Garth Reinders, John's landlord, "this is no way for the wives of National Socialists to behave." He winked at John as John turned back to the house. As soon as he felt his bed under him, John was asleep. But it seemed as if he was being shaken awake almost immediately. It was Fritz.

"What time is it?" asked John.

"Nine o'clock. Listen, John, I've been cruising around a little, and I saw a small German truck on a farmyard not fifteen minutes from here. The soldiers are all fast asleep in the barn. And I remembered what you said about keeping our eyes peeled for a good car. This is our chance! They left the key in the ignition, and the gas tank is full. All we have to do is hop in and drive it away. I even sat in it. If I had known how to drive, it would have been at Uncle Gerrit's already. Come on, man, let's go! Before they wake up!"

"Where's Josh?" John asked groggily.

"Why?" expostulated Fritz.

"We've got to check with him first."

"Oh, nuts! Well, I'll tell you what. While you get dressed, I'll go ask him. He's at Uncle Gerrit's. You come as soon as you're ready."

When John came striding up the path at Uncle Gerrit's, Fritz, Vander May and Uncle Gerrit were standing in front of the house.

"It doesn't sound like such a bad idea to me," said Vander May. "But where will we put it after we swipe it?"

Uncle Gerrit said he knew of an old barn deep in the woods. It was used for storage by the local game warden, and hardly anyone else ever went there.

"Okay, Gerrit," said Vander May, "you go ahead and wait by the woods so that you can show us the way to the barn. I'll go with John. Come on, John, we'll put on those German uniforms that your landlord has stored away for us."

"What about me?" Fritz demanded eagerly.

"You? You did your share, Fritz. You came up with the idea, didn't you? For the rest, you wait here until we get back," said Vander May.

"Aw, come on, Josh."

Fritz looked so woebegone that John felt sorry for him.

"Fritz could go ahead and check to see if the Germans are still asleep," he suggested.

"All right. Go ahead," said Vander May. "Here, wear my cap. If you're holding it in your hand when we ride up, that means it's not safe. Got that?"

"You bet! Thanks, Josh."

Fritz mounted his bike with a running start. John and Vander May followed him at an easier pace. They stopped at Reinders' place, entering as civilians and leaving as German officers. Garth was helping a fleeing N.S.M. family load their possessions when they came out of the house, and, smirking, he greeted them with the Hitler salute.

The roads were just as crowded as the day before. The exodus to the north did not seem to be letting up.

"How'd it go last night?" Vander May asked John. "Did you carry out your orders all right?"

"Well, yes, but not exactly the way you said."

"What? What do you mean? What did you do?" Vander May's voice was suddenly hard and clipped. But when John explained what had happened, his face cleared up, and he relaxed again.

"I was right about you," he said, grinning at John. "The Germans always say, orders are orders. But a man should weigh what he's doing. You made a good decision. From now on, you're my regular second-in-command. That must be the place up ahead."

The German vehicle was parked beside a large, new farmhouse. It was a green truck, and it appeared to be in pretty good shape. John was relieved to see that it was facing toward the road, so he wouldn't have to turn it around first. Fritz stood beside a nearby tree, wearing Vander May's cap; but then he removed it, wiped his forehead, and put it back on. What was that supposed to mean—safe or unsafe? Or maybe he wasn't sure? A girl came around the corner of the house carrying a milk can. She watched curiously as they rode onto the yard wearing their German uniforms. She was the only person in sight.

As usual, John had a lump of fear in his throat and a truckload in his stomach, but when he approached the vehicle, his fear dissolved, and he felt suddenly calm. Vander May took John's bike and put it in the back of the truck. John slid behind the wheel. Sure enough, the key was in the ignition! He turned it, and the needle on the gas gauge leaped to full. But where was the starter? Was it this little knob? No, that was the choke. Easy, easy. It's got to be here somewhere. Ah, this had to be it! Yes, the motor turned over and coughed.

Pump it a few times and try again. Vander May jumped in beside him, waving his revolver.

"Go!" he barked.

The engine caught, racing loudly. First gear. Why was it jerking so strangely? The hand brake! One tug and the truck leaped ahead. Someone was hollering. A German came racing out of the barn trying to head them off, but he wasn't carrying a gun. John lost sight of him as he turned onto the road.

"Heil Hitler!" shouted Vander May, laughing.

The tires bit into the dirt road as he shifted into third and floored the accelerator. It had plenty of pickup! Gravel sprayed up behind them.

"Easy does it," shouted Vander May, slapping him on the shoulder. "We're home free! Slow down or you'll hit somebody and give the German army a bad name."

"Fritz! Where's Fritz?" cried John, taking his foot off the gas.

"Right behind you," a voice blared in his ear. Fritz had jumped into the back of the truck when it had started moving and was sitting on his haunches right behind the driver's seat. "Boy, doesn't she ride great! Open it up, John, let's see what she'll do."

"What are you doing here?" asked Vander May. "I thought you were supposed to be coming back on your bike."

"You think I'm crazy? Why pedal my tail off when I can

ride? The bike's in the back. Hey, there's a bunch of other stuff back here. Boxes and duffelbags and bottles. Even a couple of rifles. We made a good haul!"

"Beautiful! We'll take a closer look at it when we get to the barn. But now keep your mouth shut, little brother. This isn't our old DKW, and I have to concentrate on my driving."

As they neared the forest, they saw Uncle Gerrit walking on the shoulder of the road. There was no one else in sight, so they stopped and pulled the old man into the cab beside Vander May. Then they drove on.

"My, my!" said Uncle Gerrit admiringly. "Say what you will, Mr. Hitler knows how to build a nice little wagon. Plenty of room for groceries and everything. Let's drive on to Berlin and thank him personally. And while we're at it, we'll pick up your dad, eh boys? Turn right up ahead. Yeah, better take it easy or you'll lose me; this isn't much of a road."

John slowed to a crawl and went bumping along over what looked like a bicycle trail. "Who knows how soon we'll be heading for Germany, the way them German troops around here are beginning to run? Hold on everybody, rough road ahead!"

Swaying and bucking, the vehicle clawed its way up the sandy trail. As they went winding between the trees, the trail gradually narrowed until branches were scraping both sides of the vehicle. Then suddenly they broke into a clearing and before them stood the barn, partly concealed by a couple of large trees. It was a perfect hiding place, thought John.

He stopped and Uncle Gerrit slid to the ground to open

the doors. Suddenly he straightened up and dashed around to the side of the barn. But he was back a moment later and motioned John to drive the truck inside.

When John climbed out inside the barn, Vander May and Uncle Gerrit were standing in a dark corner of the building looking at something. Behind a wall of branches and firewood was a bed made of straw covered with old potato sacks. In one corner lay a blue baby bonnet.

"I *thought* I heard the back door slam when I opened the front doors," said Uncle Gerrit. "Here, feel this spot; it's still warm. I caught a glimpse of her in the woods behind the barn."

"A woman?" asked John, wonderingly.

"Yes, a woman with a child. Probably escaped from that Jewish concentration camp. I'll tell you what, you guys go on home, and I'll see if I can find her. No, you better not help. You'd scare her to death in those uniforms. Fritz, *you* can come along."

Fritz and Uncle Gerrit disappeared through the back door. John lifted the bikes out of the truck.

"I wonder what's in those boxes and duffelbags," he said. "How about it, Josh, shall we take a look?"

They had reason to be pleased: four German guns, ammunition, two-dozen hand grenades, two boxes of wine, cigarettes, chocolate, a couple of bottles of French cognac, and a suitcase full of new women's clothing.

"They must have stolen this somewhere. Probably for their women back home," said Vander May. "Sorry boys, but your girls are going to be disappointed! Let's unload this stuff. We'll hide it over there, under that woodpile—except for the cigarettes and the chocolate. We'll split that among the boys. If Uncle Gerrit finds that woman who was hiding here, she'll have a ready-made wardrobe."

When they were finished, they sat down on the woodpile and shared a chocolate bar. Suddenly they heard voices, and the back door swung open. Uncle Gerrit came in carrying a young child. Behind him came Fritz and a dark, haggard-looking woman. In the darkness of the barn, she didn't see Josh and John until she was right next to them. Then she reeled back with a frightened whimper.

"You lied!" she cried to Uncle Gerrit, grabbing for her child. But Fritz restrained her.

"They're friends, lady! Honest!" Uncle Gerrit told her. "Come on, boys, say something so that she'll know you're not Germans. I thought you guys were going to leave!"

It took them some time to calm the woman. But they quickly made friends with the little girl by giving her a chocolate bar. Hungrily, she stuffed the food into her mouth, and the woman also held out an eager hand for one of the bars. When they showed her the suitcase full of clothes, she forgot her earlier fear entirely.

"It's all above board," said Uncle Gerrit. "We came by it lawfully! We requisitioned it from the German army. Go ahead, it's all yours. Right, boys? Or did you want to keep one of those cute little dresses for yourself, Josh? It would look great on you. Better than what you're wearing now."

Vander May gladly surrendered the contents of the suitcase to the young mother. Uncle Gerrit told them that her name was Mrs. Behr and that she had managed to escape when she learned that she and her child were slated for transport to Germany. That was four days ago, and they had had nothing to eat since then, except for a couple slices of bread that they had smuggled out of the camp.

Where should they take her? For the time being, she could stay at Uncle Gerrit's. John suggested that he drive her there in the German automobile, but Vander May thought the less the vehicle was seen in this vicinity the better—at least, now that the Germans would be searching for it. They could just as well take the twosome there on the back of their bikes. So an hour later, the two escapees were sitting at Uncle Gerrit's table looking on with rapt attention as the old man sliced and buttered sandwiches for them. The same evening they were moved to an address in Steve's village which Steve had provided. Many homes had suddenly become available because, with the end of the war in sight, many divers had come out of hiding and returned home. The place selected by Steve would give Mrs. Behr and her child plenty of freedom and fresh air.

That afternoon Vander May had to leave to attend a meeting from which he wouldn't return until the next day. Uncle Gerrit dropped in on the game warden to tell him about the truck parked in his barn and to arrange to put padlocks on the doors. Meanwhile, Fritz left for Groningen where he thought he could pick up some ration cards for gasoline. He returned the next morning with enough for one hundred gallons of gas. He also brought them the news that Mr. Vos had been arrested in Groningen for his black market dealings. The roads seemed to be much less crowded, Fritz observed. The big panic was apparently over. The local Nazis were starting to regain their old arrogance. Fritz had even been stopped on the road again—ironically, by the same man who had taken him in two weeks before, but this time Fritz showed his I.D.

That night the group waited in vain for Vander May to show up. The longer they waited, the more anxious they became, fearing he had been waylaid. If Uncle Gerrit had not remembered, they would have missed the radio broadcast.

The message that they had been waiting for still had not come. But the war news continued favorable. The Americans were still advancing, with heavy fighting reported around Antwerp for possession of the harbor. Nothing about Breda, however. Had the Allies reached Holland, or had the previous reports been unfounded? Or was the news being withheld to confound the enemy?

While they were debating, from outside came the sound of a bicycle bell, and a few seconds later Vander May was standing at the door, panting and perspiring, but otherwise unharmed. The group could tell from his face that he had important news. He swung a heavy satchel onto the table.

"Look what we've got here!"

Inside were two large pieces of steel resembling rails. But they were bent on one end, one of them also arching upward. On the other end were two holes so that they could be bolted to something.

"Know what those are?" asked Vander May mysteriously.

"I can guess," said John. "They look like they were made to bolt to a railroad track, one on each rail, to force the train off the tracks."

"Right! See, they deflect the wheels off to the left of the track, lifting the right wheels at the same time and thereby tipping the locomotive. On a double set of tracks, this blocks traffic in both directions. It's called a derailer! Tomorrow we try it out, boys!"

"Whoopee! Where? Where, Josh?"

"A long way from here, so we'll take the truck. Our comrades in Overijssel have asked for our help. The east-west routes seem to be especially important to the Germans; they are kept busy carrying war supplies to the western front. Let's not forget our hand grenades! I was told we might need them."

"When do we leave?" asked John.

"Early tomorrow morning. But you're not coming."

It was like getting a slap in the face, but an immediate protest was raised by the others, which made John feel a little better.

"What? John not coming! Why, Josh? We need him! Who's going to drive?"

"I can drive myself," said Vander May. "And Arend knows how to drive too. Stow it, you guys! John is second-in-command, so he has to stay here to take my place. We don't know when we'll be back, and, John, you'll run the show over here. If the message comes while we're gone, you'll have to get together a group of good men to pick up the weapons."

"And you'll also have to milk my cow," said Uncle Gerrit, "because *I'm* going with them!"

Was he serious? He looked like he meant it, but Josh slowly shook his head.

"I'm sorry, Gerrit. You're a good man, and your heart is plenty spry, but your legs aren't. Five people are enough—two to do the job, two lookouts, and one to stay with the car. So one more man will have to stay behind to help John and act as a courier, if necessary. Any volunteers?"

No one stirred.

"Then we'll draw lots," said Vander May.

He ripped a page from his datebook, tore it into five strips, and numbered them from one to four, leaving the last one blank. Then he folded them and shook them together in his cap.

"Take one," he said, holding out his cap.

Fritz's hand trembled so much that he dropped his first one back into the cap. When he unfolded his slip, he leaped into the air with a whoop. He had number one. George drew the blank slip.

"Don't cry, Georgie boy," said Uncle Gerrit, putting an arm around his shoulder. "Uncle Gerrit will take care of you. We'll feast like kings while they're gone. They'll be kicking themselves for not volunteering to stay here."

CHAPTER SIX

The next morning, after the squad had left, John and George sat glumly at the breakfast table. To stave off self-pity, they decided to cycle to Job Eising's to make preparations for the air-drop when and if it came. First, however, they stopped by Havinga's smithy to tell him about the arrest of his former guest, Mr. Vos.

"I knew he'd cause us a few headaches yet!" said Havinga, looking at John accusingly. "When they start questioning him about his I.D., I bet he'll spill everything. And then I'll get a visit from the S.D. How long ago was the fat little packrat picked up?"

John figured that it had happened maybe three days before.

"Then they should have been here by now. How come I wasn't warned sooner? Oh well, forget it. The important thing is to see that no more damage is done. I'd better make myself scarce for a while. Things were slow around the shop anyway."

"But we should know where to reach you," said John.

"Why?"

John told him about the coming air-drop. "We'd like to be able to count on your help, if necessary."

Havinga would be more than happy to lend a hand, he said. "As long as all the men involved can be trusted," he added meaningfully.

John smiled shamefacedly. The blacksmith's confidence in John's ability to judge character had been badly undermined, and John felt, deservedly so.

"You can pick your own co-workers," John told him.

Havinga said that he knew of two strong divers whom he could enlist. John told him that the men would not be briefed until necessary. A similar arrangement was made with Job Eising, who also lined up two able men.

John and George were invited to stay overnight at Eising's house. So they spent that afternoon scouting the area of the drop and even went back after dark to reassure themselves that they would be able to find their way at night. The next morning they cycled back. George stayed with Uncle Gerrit, but John put on his white jacket, fastened the baker's delivery basket to his bike, and continued to Mother's place. He got a joyful reception, and John was happy to see that Mother was looking much better. Her hope that peace was near relieved much of her anxiety.

"How long do you think it will be, John, before it's all over? Niemeyer thinks it's only a matter of a couple of weeks. We took out the flag the other day. O John, if we get Father back safe and sound, I'll be so happy! Even though we've lost everything else, I won't care—as long as

God gives me back my family! Are you sure you're quite safe at that farmer's place? And will you keep an eye on Fritz during these last days of the war?"

"These last days of the war." John didn't want to rob Mother of her hope, but as he rode back through town, he was less than confident himself. The miracle of Crazy Tuesday was no more. The N.S.M. members were as brassy as ever. Even some of those who had fled were back, and a heavily armed National Guard battalion went goose-stepping through the city streets, still singing the old Nazi marching songs. The latest news broadcasts from England made it clear that the Americans had not yet crossed the border into Holland; and, doubtless, the N.S.M. listened to the English station just as attentively as everyone else.

Just south of the Dutch border the Allies had run into fierce resistance, and the dearly bought harbor of Antwerp was useless to them, for the Germans controlled the southern tip of Holland. From there, their heavy guns could easily sink any ship trying to enter the mouth of the Scheldt River. The rapid advance of the Allies seemed to have been brought to a complete stop.

A few days later, however, John's hope that Mother might be right was revived. A little over a week after Crazy Tuesday, Maastricht was taken by the Americans. The first Dutch city had been liberated! Three days later, on Sunday, September 13, the whole country was set astir by the news of huge Allied paratroop landings around Eindhoven, Nymegen and Arnhem. The same day, the prime minister of the Dutch government-in-exile ordered all railway personnel to stop working in an attempt to halt the flow of

German reinforcements and supplies to the western front.

Uncle Gerrit had attended the afternoon worship service and, after changing into an old pair of overalls, had tromped out into the field to milk his cow. John was listening to the radio, and he dashed outside to tell him the news. The old man's eyes glistened with excitement.

"Now it's sink or swim!" he said, seizing John's arm. "But we'll make it work! Wait and see. Those railway workers are more than willing to quit. Too many of them have been getting killed by English fighter planes. But we've got to back those men up and see to it that they and their families have places to hide."

He quickly finished milking, and gave the cow an exuberant slap on the rump so that it went galloping off into the field. Then he hurried off to see a friend who worked for the railroad. The man came along with Uncle Gerrit immediately, and John and George went back to his home to pick up his wife and children. Later that night, friends and neighbors of the family moved all their furniture and possessions, so that if the Germans came to arrest the man, they would find nothing.

Two more families were helped the next morning, but the rest had already found places to hide on their own. Finding a place wasn't very difficult, for almost everyone in the country who had any room whatsoever counted it an honor to provide shelter for a striking railway worker. In one day, all the engineers, stokers, switchmen, yardmen, maintenance men, and anyone who had anything to do with the railroad disappeared. With a few exceptions, the stop-work order was observed by everyone.

One of these exceptions was an old stationmaster in a

neighboring town. Uncle Gerrit had heard that the man refused to leave his station.

"Come on, George," said John. "Let's see if we can't change the fellow's mind."

They tucked their revolvers under their belts and headed for the town where the stubborn stationmaster worked. They followed narrow bicycle trails until they got to the main highway. But they had gone only a short distance along the road when a German army vehicle roared up behind them, honking loudly. It passed, and then suddenly cut in front of them and squealed to a halt. John and George slammed on their brakes and jumped off their bikes, their hearts pounding. George was already reaching for his revolver when a grinning face peeped out from under the back tarpaulin of the truck. Fritz! Vander May jumped out of the cab, and then there followed Steve, Arend, and Jack. The whole squad was back! Of course, with all railway traffic brought to a standstill, there were no trains to derail!

Fritz jumped from the back of the truck and embraced his brother. The others also thronged around John and George, pounding them on the back, shaking hands, and all talking at the same time. John realized how much he had grown to love his comrades by how happy he was to see them all back safely.

They couldn't stay by the roadside long, however, for a couple of farmhands working in a nearby field were staring at the noisy group in astonishment. Vander May and Arend were still wearing their German uniforms.

"We'll tell you everything when we get home," said Vander May. "But where were you two going?"

When he heard about the stubborn stationmaster, he said, "Climb in. Throw your bikes in the back. We'll *all* go pay the man a visit. Okay, Arend, let's go!"

The station lay quiet and deserted under the noonday sun. Jack and Steve stayed in the back of the truck, and Arend in his German uniform remained behind the wheel. The rest went inside. Sure enough, there behind his desk sat the grizzled old man all by himself in a big, empty office.

"Two of you cut across the platform and enter from the other side," Vander May ordered softly.

Then with George standing behind him, he knocked on the wicket. The man looked up and slowly came to the counter. Vander May saluted. "A third class ticket to Amsterdam, please," he asked.

The man stared at him with raised eyebrows.

"I'm sorry, sir," he replied. "I very much doubt whether there will be any trains going to Amsterdam today."

"Then what are *you* doing here?" demanded Vander May.

"What am I doing here? You, a German officer, have to ask that? I belong here! This is my post! I've been stationmaster here for twenty years. You don't think I'm going to walk out just for some silly strike do you?"

"Yes, I do. Because I'm not a German, but a Dutch soldier, and I expect every loyal Dutchman to obey his government. Now, come on out of there!" Vander May suddenly thrust his pistol through the wicket, and the man jumped backward in fright, right into the arms of John and Fritz.

"Bring him to the truck," ordered Vander May.

"But what about my wife?" wailed the old man.

"Where is your wife?"

"Upstairs. We live here above the station."

"All right, lead the way upstairs. I'll give you five minutes to pack a few clothes. The rest you can pick up later."

The entrance to the upstairs apartment was around the front of the building. With trembling fingers, the old man fished his keys out of his pocket, unlocked the door, and led them up a narrow stairway. At the top they were met by a sweet-looking old lady with a bun in her hair. She didn't seem the least bit frightened or surprised.

"Do you really belong to the underground?" she asked. "My, how exciting. See, honey, I told you they'd come!"

"I'm sorry, madam, but you'll have to hurry," interrupted John. "You have only five minutes to pack a suitcase."

"Oh, don't worry. I'm all packed already, my dear boy," she told him, laughing. "I've even put my cat in her basket. Here, you may carry it. The suitcases are over there. Come on, Bert, take off that railroad cap and put on your coat. You're forever catching colds."

"Did you have a place in mind where you wanted to go?" Vander May asked her, politely.

"But of course!" she said. "To my niece in Assen. You'll take us, won't you? The little ones will stare their eyes out!"

They could hardly refuse such a charming old lady, and the trip became a jolly outing. The excited wife sat in front between Vander May and Arend. To her great delight, two Guardsmen standing by the road to inspect vehicles snapped to attention and gave a straight-arm salute as the truck went by. When the old couple had been dropped off, the stationmaster's wife gave John a hearty kiss for carrying her suitcases.

"My, my, look at him blush!" she teased. "You're a sweet boy. Thank you very much—all of you. Drive carefully now. Goodbye!"

On the way back, five of the squad were dropped off in the vicinity of Uncle Gerrit's house, while Vander May and Arend took the vehicle back to its hiding place. They joined the rest of the group about an hour later. The evening was spent recounting their adventures. They had derailed three trains—one with the derailer, one by setting a railway bridge a little awry, and another by blowing the engine off the tracks with a bundle of hand grenades.

They had tied several grenades together and jammed them under a rail, fastening a string to one of the pins. When that one went off, all the others would explode too, Vander May had assured them. They tied on about one hundred and fifty meters of string, but for added security they attached several shoelaces and handkerchiefs and then dug a deep hole to provide themselves with cover. After that, it was only a matter of waiting for a train to come along.

Fritz and Steve had hidden themselves farther along the railroad grade to watch for the track patrol. If he came along and discovered their explosives, they were to jump him and take him prisoner. A patrol did show up, but he walked along the other track and noticed nothing. So they let him pass, as Vander May had ordered.

The squad waited for several hours and was beginning to

fear that they would have to blow up the tracks without a train, when they heard a faint, far-off rumble that grew louder and louder. In the early morning twilight, they could see it coming—an enormously long supply train chugging laboriously toward them. Fritz and Steve came running and dove into the foxhole. Vander May had both hands clamped on the string, and he waited until the locomotive was almost on top of the grenades.

"You should have seen it, Uncle Gerrit!" said Jack. "I was really kind of skeptical of the plan, so I had my head above the edge of the hole. First, there was a flash so bright it hurt my eyes, and then a bang that made my ears ring for half an hour afterwards. I fell backwards into the hole, stunned, and dirt and gravel rained down on us. But I had seen the locomotive stagger. Then it rose like an elephant getting up on its hind legs. When I peeked over the edge of the foxhole again, it was lying on its side diagonally across the tracks. Three or four boxcars had also crashed down the embankment. There was a large crater where we had planted the grenades."

"What about the engineer?" asked Uncle Gerrit. "How was he? He must have been a Dutchman."

They had no way of knowing. When the dust settled, dozens of German soldiers came spilling out of the remaining cars. All they thought about was getting out of there.

"We did discuss it ahead of time, Uncle Gerrit," said Vander May, "and it grieved us deeply that we had to endanger the lives of some of our fellow countrymen, but we saw no other way. So we were sure glad when we heard about the strike."

The most exciting part of the expedition, however, came on the way back. They had taken the shortest route home, which led near the huge German camp at Ommen. A few kilometers before Ommen, they passed a German army truck parked on the shoulder of the road, a truck very similar to their own. An officer standing by the truck tried to wave them down, but, of course, they had no intention of stopping. The other vehicle then came after them, and a high speed chase followed. When they neared the German camp, they had only about a fifty-meter lead on the other truck. As they rounded a curve, suddenly there were four Germans on the road ahead signaling them to stop.

Vander May didn't even slow down. He just thrust his head out the window and yelled in German, "I can't stop! My brakes are shot!"

The Germans had raised their rifles, but they lowered them when they heard Vander May. As the truck passed them, however, they saw Fritz and Jack in the back clutching their revolvers. They were keeping an eye on the truck behind. So one of the soldiers opened fire on them. But the others turned their rifles on the second truck, apparently assuming that they were part of the same gang. The first soldier put a couple of holes in their tarpaulin, but the others were better shots. Fritz and Jack saw the pursuing truck go careening off the road and slam into a tree.

As they told the story, the young men got excited all over again, and Steve whooped with laughter as he pictured what those soldiers must have looked like when they discovered that they had fired on their own comrades.

"All I can say is, you guys had more than your share of the breaks," said John, looking worriedly at his younger brother. He was thinking of his promise to Mother, that he would keep an eye on Fritz. What if he had to bring her the message someday that Fritz . . . . He shuddered to think of it.

"I'd prefer to say that you fellows were miraculously spared," said Uncle Gerrit. "And we ought to thank God for your safe return. And don't go counting on such miracles to happen *every* time. You guys have got to be more careful!"

"John!" he cried suddenly. "We're missing the news!"

The war was still going well for the Allies. American forces had struck northward out of Belgium and made contact with the parachute troops around Eindhoven. Now they were pressing on in the direction of Nymegen, thus driving a wedge into the German forces in Brabant. General Montgomery's strategy was clear: to seize the bridges over the main rivers with parachute troops and to make a daring, lightning attack along a small front. If his plan worked, the way would be open for the victorious Allied armies to advance into Germany, and Holland's liberation would not be far off.

The next day, Vander May told them all to take a few days off. They needed it, and soon, perhaps, they would need all their strength and alertness; for after they received their weapons, Vander May thought they might even be ordered to join the Inland Battle Forces to launch an attack on the German rear. Vander May himself decided to join John at the Reinders' farm.

During their short vacation, they suddenly got a call from Havinga, informing them that their plow was ready. John had to think twice before he remembered what the code words meant. Mr. Vos? But wasn't he in jail?

"You'll just have to go over there and see what's up," said Vander May. "Why don't I go with you? The man wouldn't have called if he didn't need you."

It was late evening by the time they reached the village. Vander May first cycled past Havinga's place a couple of times, but he saw nothing suspicious. Then both of them carefully approached the house from the back, parking their bikes against the blacksmith shop. Before they got to the house, the door opened and Havinga stepped outside. He must have been watching for them.

"He's inside," he told them. "Be careful! I don't trust him."

"Who? Vos?"

"Who else? Your information about him being in jail must have been wrong."

"Did you ask him about it?"

"Not me. I pretended I got a bloody nose. He started asking all kinds of questions. He wanted your address and also the address of the man who fixed his I.D. He said he wanted to talk to you on underground business. Some underground worker *he'd* make, that windbag! I told him you were going to be stopping by today, so he's been waiting for you. I really don't know what to do about the two-faced little jerk!"

"Leave him to us," said Vander May. "Let's go, John. I want to sound out your charming little friend. We'll go along with him at first, just to see what he says."

Mr. Vos sprang to his feet when they entered the room and rushed forward to shake John's hand. For a moment, John thought that the man was going to embrace him.

"Ah, it does my heart good to see my young friend and savior!" he cried exuberantly. "Is this a friend of yours, John? Well, any friend of John's is a friend of mine. I suppose you belong to the underground too, eh?"

"Carl's the name," said Vander May.

"Vos," said Mr. Vos. "V as in victory, O as in orange . . . ." The same old joke, but John interrupted him.

"You can forget that 'savior' bit," John said. "The Germans would hardly have shot you."

"That's what you think!" exclaimed Vos. "Obviously, you've never been arrested by them. They're devils once they get their hands on you!"

"Did they ever get their hands on you?" asked Vander May.

"Me? No! Why do you ask?"

"Well, because you said they were devils once they . . . ."

"Oh, no. They'll never get their hands on me! But I've talked to some people who *did* get picked up by them."

He had spent time in a German jail, John was convinced. According to Fritz, his wife had said as much to the neighbors. But then how had he got out so quickly? And why wouldn't he admit that he had been arrested? A good thing Josh had come along. As an ex-policeman, he knew how to ask questions.

What were they talking about now? Oh, Vos was just asking Vander May if he was a diver, since he had given only his first name.

"Yes," said Vander May, "and I'm also in the resistance, in a special branch of the resistance, in fact."

"Oh, really?" Vos asked nosily. "What do you do?"

"I'll tell you that only after we get to know you better," Vander May told him. "Did you plan to become one of us?"

"How did you know?" cried Vos. "That's precisely why I came here!"

"But why us?" Vander May continued in a friendly tone of voice.

"Well, because I know two of you already. It isn't the easiest organization to get into, you know."

"No, I can understand that," said Vander May. "But, tell me, why didn't you try to join the group in Groningen? That's your home town, isn't it? You must know a lot more than two people there. Excuse me for prying this way, Mr. Vos, but we have to be very careful about recruiting new members. As you know, we have to guard against traitors seeking to infiltrate our organization. So, I repeat, why not Groningen?"

"You see, I figure I'm too well known around there. That could be dangerous too."

"And what kind of work did you want to do?"

"Well, whatever you fellows do."

"What do you *think* we do?"

Mr. Vos started laughing. "This almost sounds like an interrogation."

"That's precisely what it is," said Vander May. The blacksmith's wife had just brought them coffee, and Vander May waited until she left the room. "Before we take you aboard, Mr. Vos, we have to know all about you. Are you armed?"

"Yes, I've got a revolver."

"Let's have a look at it."

Vos reached into the pocket of his suit coat and put a small, rusty pistol on the table. Vander May picked it up, checked it over—it was loaded—and put in into his own pocket.

"Anything else?"

"No," said Vos, "but . . . but . . . ."

"Yes? What is it?"

"Could I please have my gun back? It's mine!"

"In a little while. Now empty your pockets, please. Put everything on the table," Vander May continued in the same friendly tone.

But Mr. Vos was becoming uneasy. He was beginning to sweat. Small beads formed on his forehead and upper lip. His coffee remained untouched.

"You don't object, do you Mr. Vos, to our finding out as much as possible about you? Or do you have something to hide?"

Mr. Vos went through all his pockets, placing everything on the table in front of Vander May—a pack of cigarettes, a pocket knife, a handkerchief, a small newspaper, a bunch of keys, and then, hesitantly, a wallet.

"Would you search Mr. Vos a minute, John? We want to be sure that nothing has been overlooked, right, Mr. Vos?"

"Remember, I'm ticklish," Vos said, laughing nervously.

John went through all the pockets a second time, coming up with a small appointment book. Vander May examined each object at his leisure but seemed to find nothing remarkable. Vos picked up his handkerchief and swabbed his forehead and balding cranium.

"Are you hot?" asked Vander May. "I didn't think it

was that warm in here. Everything seems to be in order. I guess you can put these things back into your pockets. Oh, just one thing! This number in your appointment book—is it a phone number? Look, this one. It has a little house drawn next to it."

"Here, let me see."

Vos took the little book, looked at the number and laughed. "Doesn't mean a thing, I assure you," he said, swallowing. "Sometimes I just sit and doodle. Doesn't mean a thing. Just mindless scribblings."

In a nervous spasm, he ripped the page out of the booklet and, wadding it up, quickly stepped to the stove and tossed it into the fire. Vander May gave John a very pointed look.

"Yes, sir," said Vos. "I can understand your being cautious, but you've nothing to fear from me. Just ask John, here. He'll vouch for me. He knows me. Right, John?"

He gave John a quick wink, but John pretended not to notice. "Yes," he answered, "I know you Mr. Vos. I know, for example, that you spent some time in jail recently. Why don't you tell us how you got out so fast."

Vos looked as if he were going to faint. He closed his eyes and took a couple of deep breaths. But he recovered quickly.

"In jail? Me? How did you . . . ? What makes you think . . . ."

"Just a minute, Mr. Vos," interrupted Vander May. "Before you go on, let me show you this."

He had pulled out his wallet and, taking out some papers, he handed them to Vos. They were phony S.D.

documents describing Vander May as an S.D. detective.

"I told you I was in a special branch of the underground, but you may have misunderstood what I meant by that."

Now Vos was completely unsettled. He looked from one to the other in evident consternation.

"So you're with the S.D.?" he simpered.

"As you see."

"Him too?" he asked, nodding at John.

"Yes, him too. Quite recently, as a matter of fact. For a time he was foolish enough to fight for a lost cause, just like you. But one day we picked up Mr. De Jong, and it didn't take us long to convince him that he was on the wrong side. And now Mr. Vos, I'm afraid you're in the same position. You're under arrest. Yes, we've tricked you. Trying to join the underground, you'll find, is just as serious an offense as actually being a member. You've walked right into our trap!"

For a moment Vos looked dubiously from Vander May to John, but then he started to laugh uproariously. He was obviously relieved.

"Into your trap!" he guffawed. "You're right! Yes, and you walked into mine. Hee, hee! The same thing happened to me as to him," he said, pointing to John, "and now I'm working for the S.D. too. Isn't that hilarious! Ha, ha, ha!"

Vander May laughed right along with the fat little comedian, and John tried to join in too, but it sounded a little hollow, even to his own ears.

"Quite a coincidence," said Vander May. "You have proof of what you say, of course?"

"Well, I don't have papers like you do, of course," answered Vos. "But if you call that phone number in my appointment book . . . . You recognized that number, didn't you? That's why you asked about it!"

"Yes. It was the number of S.D. headquarters in Groningen."

"Right. All you have to do is give them a call and they'll confirm my story. Let me tell you how it happened."

Vos, it seemed, had been wholly taken in by the false S.D. papers and by Vander May's performance. He took a couple quick swallows of coffee, and then he launched into his story. One day when he was sitting in a café in Groningen, he had been recognized by the man who had handcuffed him in the train. Because he had again been carrying ration cards and that old revolver, which he was hoping to sell, he had received harsh treatment at the hands of the S.D. But when they had discovered that he was no threat to the German regime, his S.D. captor had suddenly done an about-face and offered him a job.

"Right!" said Vander May, still playing his role. "A man has got to live! What do they pay you? I get close to three hundred a month."

Vos grimaced. "I work on a commission. Hundred guilders a head, I was promised."

"Hear that, John? The two of us would have brought our friend here two hundred guilders. And they called him a harmless rascal in Groningen!"

John was having difficulty controlling himself. He thought of Father and Fritz, of Carl Van Bergen, Uncle Henry and Joe—all of whom had put their lives on the line for freedom and justice, for the very things that this man was selling for a few hundred guilders. He itched to grab

Vos by the throat. He no longer trusted his voice, so he kept quiet.

"Listen," said Vos, "perhaps we can work together. You guys let me bring in whoever you catch, and I'll give you a cut of my commission. I'm on the trail of the guy who fixed me up with a phony I.D. And I suppose you've already picked up the farmer who brought me here. He was obviously in with them. And what about our host?"

He almost whispered the last words, eyeing the door to the kitchen.

"Did you already report him to the S.D.?" asked Vander May. John felt that his lips were trembling. Vander May was also struggling to control himself.

"You kidding?" snorted Vos. "Then they'd have picked him up right away, and I knew he could lead me to others."

"Smart thinking, Vos. You're a regular fox, you are! Well, John, what do you say about our cunning little friend? What do we do?"

John had to clear his throat before speaking. His voice trembled with rage and contempt.

"I think we don't have much choice. There's only one thing we can do!"

"I'm afraid you're right," agreed Vander May. "Fetch Havinga, and tell him to bring some strong rope."

Vos didn't immediately catch on that the rope was meant for him. In fact, he didn't really believe what was happening until he lay bound hand and foot and gagged in the woodshed behind the smithy. The gag had become necessary to silence his begging and wailing.

The blacksmith was in favor of bringing swift and harsh judgment on the man that same night, and he volunteered

to carry it out himself. Although it would have been the safest thing to do, Vander May hesitated. At John's suggestion, it was decided that no judgment be executed until they got Uncle Gerrit's advice. So Vander May left late that evening to fetch the old man and returned with him early the next morning in the German army truck.

Uncle Gerrit had also donned a German uniform for the trip, and despite the solemnity of the occasion, John burst out laughing when the bow-legged old man climbed out of the truck. Now that Hitler was drawing on his last reserves, some quite old soldiers were showing up in German uniform, but he'd never seen one that old!

Uncle Gerrit opposed the death sentence.

"We have to be ready to give an account of everything we do not only to God but perhaps also to a court of law after this is all over," he warned. "And I wouldn't be able to sleep if we shot this man. He hasn't really betrayed anyone yet, at least, not that we know of. Sure, we know that for a price he'd turn almost anyone over to the Germans, given the chance. But we'll see to it that he never gets the chance. From the looks of it, the war will be over before long. I propose that we lock the man up until the end of the war."

"Then you'd better lock him up real good!" the blacksmith said darkly. "And keep him out of my sight!"

Two hours later Mr. Vos was locked up in a root cellar concealed under a haystack on an isolated farm. They made arrangements that he would be well cared for, that he would be let out for air and exercise every evening. He would be watched over by a Jewish diver who had escaped from Westerbork and by a large German shepherd. Samuel, the guard, was given Vos's old revolver and told to shoot if the prisoner made the slightest attempt to escape.

"Remember," Vander May told him, "if you botch your job, all our lives aren't worth a wooden nickel!"

"You think I learned nothing in that camp, maybe?" said Samuel. "I should forget my wife and kids who were sent to Poland? That snake won't get out of that cellar as long as the war lasts, even if it's another ten years!"

"Well, don't worry, it won't be that long," Vander May assured him. "It'll be over any day now."

"Sure," replied Samuel skeptically, "that's what we've been telling each other for years."

CHAPTER SEVEN

The war news continued to be good for several days. Nymegen was liberated, and the bridge over the Meuse miraculously fell into American hands undamaged. The story was that a boy had climbed the girders of the bridge during the night and disconnected all the charges that the Germans had put under it. Now the road was open to Arnhem, where English parachute troops were locked in fierce battle with strong enemy forces. The bridge at Arnhem was crucial to the Allied invasion of Holland. If the Allies were able to capture the bridge, nothing would be able to stop their victorious advance into the rest of the country. But if they didn't, the war in Holland was far from over.

Every day the group gathered around the radio in suspense to await the latest news from England. But day after day went by without an Allied victory. It was taking too long! Slowly the boys began to realize that the news they longed to hear wasn't coming. Half of Arnhem had been destroyed by the fighting, and all of its inhabitants had been driven out into the countryside—all in vain. Ten days after the paratroop landings, it was obvious that the strike at Arnhem had failed. The Americans were not able to break through to the city, and most of the English paratroopers had been killed or captured. Just a small group escaped across the Rhine during the night.

Incredible as it seemed, the Germans still had a strong grip on the land, and they seemed determined to prove that they were still in control. The searches for Jews and other divers began again, and everywhere people were being arrested who had become too open in their anti-German sentiments. The Nazis also tried to entice the railway workers back to work by promising them double wages and extra rations, but only a few succumbed to the temptation. Then the Germans threatened that no food would be shipped to the large cities in the west of the country unless the trains began running again. But that didn't produce any results either. The few trains that moved were manned by German workers.

The National Guard also reappeared on the roads, more obnoxious than ever. You couldn't cycle very far in any direction without being stopped for a check. But the work of the resistance had to go on, for there were now more divers than ever waiting for money and ration cards. So the group kept going out. Fritz was on the road almost every day, his accordion slung across his back. His youth and brazen good humor seemed to take him through everything.

One day when he had to deliver a revolver, he hid it in the bottom of a flower pot and planted a big geranium right on top of it. Once again he was on his way to a wedding, with the flower as a present for the bride. Dressed in bib overalls and carrying a manure fork, Steve put on his best farmboy manner and was hardly given a second glance by the inspectors. John was also fairly safe in his baker's outfit, with a handful of flour sprinkled on his hair. But one day George made it just by the skin of his neck.

He was on his way to Uncle Gerrit's house with a satchel full of ration cards, illegal newspapers, and forged I.D.'s, so he didn't want to risk being searched. When he saw two National Guardsmen on the road ahead, one of whom was carrying a shotgun, he slowed down, and as he was passing, he punched the man with the gun so hard that he tumbled backward into the ditch. Then George sped away on his bike, bent low over the handlebars. He was almost a kilometer down the road before he heard the shotgun blast behind him and something stung his neck. Half an hour later, Uncle Gerrit had picked five pellets from the back of his neck, dropping them one by one into the palm of George's hand.

"Maybe you'd like to save them, kind of like souvenirs," he said.

"Of course," said George, rubbing his sore neck. "And if I ever run into that guy again, I'll return them. It's against my principles to accept gifts from Nazis."

"Come, come," said Uncle Gerrit grinning, "not so proud. He was just trying to return your kindness. After all, you gave him something to remember you by too."

Thus they joked whenever they were all safely back together again. But on other days, when they had nothing to do and when the news continued to be depressing, Uncle Gerrit had a rough time keeping their spirits up.

Near the beginning of October, a resistance group ambushed a German car near the village of Putten, killing one German officer and wounding another. Two other men escaped. Early the next day—it was Sunday morning—German soldiers surrounded the whole town. Then they went from house to house herding the women and children into the church and the men into the school. About one hundred homes were burned to the ground. The following day, almost all the men of the village were loaded into cattle trucks and transported to the transit camp at Amersfoort and from there to various German camps. The village of Putten was virtually emptied of its menfolk.

"Was their resistance work justifiable in the face of such staggering cost?" the squad members asked themselves. "Wouldn't it be better to stop aggravating the Germans, now that they were striking back so viciously?" As they discussed the issue, Fritz suddenly came up with the idea of cycling south and swimming across the Rhine during the night to join the Americans in the liberated zone. If Vander May had given him the okay, Fritz would have taken off immediately. But Vander May knew better.

"We can't do them much good over there," he argued. "They have plenty of men. We belong here! All resistance groups have received orders to stay in their own localities. From now on, we'll be more careful than ever in order not to rouse the enemy to reprisals. Not until we get our weapons and the Allies are close will we come into the open."

"Weapons?" sneered Fritz. "You still counting on that air-drop?"

Despite his skepticism, Fritz was with the others,

listening to the radio again that evening at quarter to nine. The southern province of Brabant was slowly being cleared of all Germans. The island of Walcheren, in the southwest corner of the country, had been almost completely flooded by the English dam-busters in an attempt to drive the Germans out. Nevertheless, the Germans were putting up a tenacious struggle over Vlissingen. Allied mine sweepers lay ready to go in and clean out the mouth of the Scheldt River so that the port of Antwerp could be put into service to receive new troops and supplies.

The announcer on Radio Orange closed with words of encouragement for those still in occupied territory: "Don't give up! We will endure! There is but one new order—the order of resistance!"

"It's easy for him to talk, sitting across the channel," muttered Fritz.

Then followed the Belgian broadcast, which was of little interest to the group, since Belgium had already been liberated; but they were waiting for the special announcements that followed. Tonight there were nine of them. The announcer said, "This is how Napoleon did it. I repeat, this is how Napoleon did it. The bill is not yet paid . . . . It's time to get out of bed." They all sounded like nonsense, except of course to those anxiously waiting for the code word. And then into the quiet room came the long-awaited message: "John has made a good catch."

First the room remained completely silent as the announcer repeated the message. Then they were all on their feet at the same time. They grabbed each other, Fritz embracing Uncle Gerrit, and George and Jack dancing around the table. Even Steve lost his usual calm demeanor and jumped up on a chair, shouting, "There's but one new order: the order of resistance!" Yes, they would endure as the announcer had said. They would never give up!

They had to leave as soon as possible.

"No thanks, Uncle Gerrit, no time for another cup of coffee! Save it until tomorrow morning when we get back."

"What's the weather like tonight?"

"Blustery, almost stormy. We'll probably get rain squalls all night long."

"Raincoats on everybody, and take along that old tarpaulin to sit under when we're there. Boots on and revolvers in the pockets of your raincoats. If the National Guard tries to stop us on the road, we'll shoot our way through!"

Ten minutes later they were leaving the yard, riding their bicycles in single file. John led the way because he knew the trails through the woods better than anyone else. Although it wasn't raining yet, the cloud cover was thick and the night was extremely dark. Each rider could just make out the shape of the man in front of him. Occasionally, one of them would lose the narrow trail and sink into the muddy surface beside it. Once Steve hit a rut along the trail and fell across the path so that Jack and George crashed into him and also went for a spill. But they got up and pedaled on, and about an hour later they were knocking on Eising's door to roust him out of bed. He came running to the door in his underwear, and he wanted to get dressed to go with them. But that wasn't necessary, said Vander May. They had stopped only to warn him to be prepared to receive them after they had picked up the weapons.

Half an hour later, they were standing at the edge of the field where the air-drop was to take place. They hid their bicycles in the underbrush, and Vander May ran them all through their paces. Jack, George, Arend, and Fritz would all operate signal lights.

"Come on, fellows, hustle! It's past eleven, and the air-plane could be here any time. Which way's the wind? From there—northwest. Jack, you stand here with the red light. George, one hundred meters straight down with the white light, and then Arend, another hundred meters further down with the second red light. Make sure you're all in a straight line!

"Fritz, you go out sixty meters straight left of the middle light. You'll send the signal: short, short, long; short, short, long. Try it over here under the tarpaulin. Yes, that's good. That's the position you'll each take when we hear the air-plane coming, got that? But don't begin signaling until you hear me hoot like an owl, like this: whoo-o-oo, whoo-o-oo. Keep your flashlights with you, but don't mess with them! Now, everybody come over here, and we'll see how quickly we can get to our positions."

They practiced until they had their parts down perfectly. Then all they could do was wait. They huddled together by a low stone wall and listened to the throaty rumble of English bombers passing far to the north. The sky had cleared. Small shreds of cloud scudded by the thin sliver of moon that nicked the sky. To the northeast, searchlights spooked back and forth across the horizon between bright flashes of antiaircraft fire. John supposed that it was Bremen, but George thought that it had to be Emden.

"Bremen would be farther to the right," he said. "Hamburg is right about there, and . . . ."

A thud and a yelp from nearby.

". . . and Josh is right about there," finished George, chuckling.

Vander May had been scouting the field by himself and had tripped over a big stone.

"If I ever again get a voice in running this country," he grumbled, "the first thing on the program will be to get all these lousy rocks picked up! Here's the first one."

He dropped the one that he had tripped over beside the low stone wall and sat down on it. The others, too, began to make themselves comfortable, sitting down next to him on clumps of grass or on the tarpaulin. The night became very still. In the shelter of the stone wall, the chill wind didn't bother them. Too bad they couldn't smoke. They stared into the blackness, listening to the wind whispering in the bushes and trees, their eyes continually drawn to the stars fixed high overhead, bright and clear. The calm and peace of the night seeped into them. The war seemed far away, like an unbelievable dream.

At first they kept their ears perked for the sound of the plane, but when the slender sickle of the moon sank down below the trees, they relaxed. Steve fell asleep, his chin resting on his knees. John stood up, stretched, yawned, and began pacing back and forth to restore his circulation. Brrr! He had become chilled and stiff, sitting still so long. Jack started telling a joke.

"Have you heard the one about the Dutch laborer who was being sent to Germany to work? His wife asked him to write and tell her what it was really like, without hiding anything. But that wasn't possible, of course, because the German censors wouldn't let anything get through that reflected badly on the Nazi regime. So they had a plan. Everything written in black ink would be true, and everything written in red would mean precisely the opposite.

"Well, a few weeks later, the wife got her first letter. She opened it, and to her relief, everything was written in black. It was a glowing letter! The work was a cinch, short hours, the food delicious and plentiful, beautiful housing, and no trouble from English bombers. She was delighted with the news, of course. When she got to the end of the letter, however, there was a P.S. 'I have only one small complaint, dear wife. There's no red ink in the camp'!"

George, too, had a joke to tell, about the zinc coins minted by the Germans.

"A N.S.M. man was collecting for the Nazi charity, Winter Relief, in a Rotterdam slum. Old lady Vander Itch on the third floor opened her window and dropped a piece of zinc eavestrough on his head. 'Why don't you cut a few quarters out of that!' she hollered down."

"I've got a riddle," said Fritz. "The war is over, peace has just been declared, and a big plane lands in the capital. The door opens and out steps a dignified, gray-haired old lady. Guess who?"

"What a dumb riddle, Queen Wilhelmina, of course."

"Nope!" said Fritz. "Princess Beatrix." Beatrix was the princess who had been born two years before the beginning of the war.

The others thought it was a sick, cynical joke. "How come so pessimistic, Fritz? You think a little river like the

Rhine is going to stop the Americans for sixty years? Sixty days at most!"

"Sure, by next spring I bet we'll be free men again."

"Yeah, and what are we going to do then? We'll be unemployed."

"Assuming we're still around."

"Don't be so morbid! Of course, we'll still be around. You've got to think positively! I know what *I* plan to do."

They all had their own dreams. George had a girl and hoped to get married. The first thing facing John after the war was finishing his studies and writing his exams. He had heard that students whose studies had been interrupted by the war were going to be given special exams. Steve said that he wanted to go to Indonesia as a soldier and help liberate it from the Japanese. Fritz thought that he would go along to help free his uncle and aunt from the Japanese concentration camp. Whatever their plans, they all pictured the future as a time of fulfilled dreams, a life without fear and anxiety, with plenty of food and drink, with prosperity and stores full of new goods at fair prices, with freedom to travel wherever you wished.

"I'm afraid you're going to be disappointed, fellows," said Vander May. "Shall I give you a more likely picture? A completely impoverished, plundered nation with rationing for years to come and taxes like we've never seen before! And all those stuffed shirts who dropped out of sight during the war will come oozing back out of the woodwork and climb back into their velvet seats . . . ."

"Then we'll drive them back into their holes with our revolvers!" cried Fritz.

"I'm afraid not, Fritz," said Vander May. "When the

whole country is free again and the government is back, we'll all turn in our weapons and behave like quiet, law-abiding citizens. And if the government does things not to our liking, all we can do is try to convince one another that policies ought to be changed."

They talked about the future for a long time, finally coming to a consensus that freedom would not usher in a paradise. Nevertheless, it was worth fighting for, even if it were only to be out from under the tyrannical yoke of the Nazis! The freedom to believe and speak and act according to one's conscience was somehow bound up with the meaning of life itself. What was life without it?

But here they were, sitting in a field in enemy-occupied territory with their freedom far from won. It was past three in the morning, and the airplane that they were waiting for still hadn't showed up.

"If I let my girl wait this long," said George, with a sigh, "she'd tell me to forget it. What about yours, John?"

"I guess!" said John. And that was all. His thoughts focused on Rita. He hadn't seen her for several weeks, and the last visit had lasted less than an hour. She had made a brief stopover at Uncle Gerrit's on her way south to pick up a Jewish child. She was busy with resistance work again. He hoped that nothing would happen to her before the end of the war. She simply had to make it! What would he do if she . . . . No, better not even think of it.

All that one could do was hope for the best, also with regard to Father. Mother was worried again because the trains weren't running, so Father wasn't getting his food packages. The only thing to do was to hope, hope that he'd survive. And pray! Yes, that too! They went together: hope and pray.

John looked up at the stars and at the limitlessness beyond. "O God, spare Father, and spare all of us for one another," he said inaudibly, and he held that thought until he saw the whole family back together, including Rita. He dozed off thinking of her.

When Vander May woke him up, the eastern horizon was already showing the first light of the new day. Chilled to the bone, he stumbled along after the others to the Eising farmhouse, where they were met by the smell of pancakes and coffee. The English might have forgotten them, but not Mrs. Eising. After breakfast, Vander May returned to Uncle Gerrit's house, just in case a message had come for him there, while the rest of the squad crawled up into the haymow and slept until late afternoon.

When they awoke, Vander May was back. Again that night the code words were broadcasted, and again the men trudged out into the field after dark. The wind had settled down, but it began to drizzle, and it didn't stop until daybreak. They returned to their hosts, dripping water all over the kitchen floor. Mrs. Eising insisted that they take the warm beds that the Eising family had just vacated, and she took their clothes and hung them to dry around the kitchen stove.

The third night was beautiful; the air was still, and the sky was clear, but it wasn't at all cold. However, by four o'clock nothing had showed, and they resigned themselves to another fruitless night. They were just pulling their bikes out of the bushes when Vander May yelled, "The lights! Grab your lights, boys! It's the plane. They're here!"

The dark shadow of the droning airplane came gliding low over the trees. Those who were manning the flashlights ran out into the field, shining their lights up into the sky. The big machine roared by directly overhead and disappeared into the darkness. They could still hear it. The sound of the engines changed; it was banking! It was coming back! Now they had the lamps neatly lined up—red, white, red, with Fritz flashing the morse code signal off to the side. The airplane came thundering back less than two hundred meters from the ground, the noise reverberating through their bodies. And then it was gone again.

But what was that noise? It sounded like the clash and clatter of metal on metal. Against the clear night sky, John saw three parachutes floating downward, lower and lower until they disappeared into the dark countryside. He ran toward them with Steve at his side. Behind him he heard Vander May shouting, "Keep signaling! Don't stop!" Again the sound of the powerful engines approached, and three more parachutes opened not far overhead. He could hear the cargo hitting the ground. What if one of those heavy boxes dropped right on top of him? Without breaking stride, he veered off to the side of the field just as the airplane made its third pass. Then it flew on, heading west.

Vander May hollered something, but no one was listening. They were all running out into the field and their shouts came from every direction as they discovered their longed-for booty. John found two big baskets standing side by side in the grass, half covered by a parachute. Baskets? Why baskets? Fritz came running up and shone his light on

them. On the side of the baskets was a red plate with the number 38. John untied one of the parachutes and began folding it neatly. But suddenly Fritz poked him and pointed to the edge of the field. There in the black shadows of the trees, two lights were flashing: dot, dot, dash; dot, dot, dash. And then a voice shouted, "John has made a good catch!"

Vander May joined them. He didn't know what was going on either. They walked toward the woods, their revolvers in their hands.

"Who is it?" shouted Vander May.

"Friends," the voice replied in English. "Over here!" There could be little doubt that the man was English.

The boys rushed to the Englishman from all sides. They found two parachutists, who had jumped with the air-drop. John had indeed made a good catch! The one, Captain MacBaf, was an instructor to teach the squad how to use their new weapons. The other was a young Dutchman called Rudi, who had come along to act as translator and radioman. There was much hand-shaking and back-slapping as everyone in the group pushed forward to touch these two men who had been in England only two hours ago. The visitors produced cigarettes and chocolate bars—English cigarettes and real chocolate!

"What's in those baskets?" Fritz asked Rudi.

"My radio and other supplies."

"More supplies? You mean more cigarettes and chocolate? Man, we'll get spoiled rotten!"

"No smoking here, fellows," warned Vander May. "And please keep your voices down. We've got to be careful, Captain! John, you escort our two guests to the farm, and tell Eising to bring his horse and wagon. Take your bike so you can come back faster. We need all the help we can get to haul this stuff onto one pile. Let's get started!"

When John got back, everyone was still working hard. The weapons were packed in long, heavy metal canisters. It took all their combined strength to haul them alongside the baskets. Job Eising had to make two trips with his wagon; otherwise it would have been too heavy for the soft country road. The sky was already starting to pale by the time that they were done and had all their supplies safely stashed in a root cellar which Mr. Eising had reserved for that purpose.

After breakfast no one had the slightest inclination to go to bed. There were English cigarettes, and many questions to ask Rudi and the captain. But Vander May took John and Steve back to the air-drop site to search the whole area one more time. They found a flashlight and a glove, and in the trees, a whole canister that had come down against a tree trunk and split wide open. Hand grenades and parts of weapons were spread around for several meters. They collected it all and buried it under branches and leaves, to be picked up after dark. Next time, said Vander May, they would have to set up more toward the middle of the field.

When they got back to the house, Captain MacBaf was walking around the farm with Mr. Eising. The captain owned a farm in Scotland, and he displayed a lively interest in Eising's farming methods. The farmhouse was filled from cellar to attic with the smell of English cigarettes. Rudi was already up in the attic with his radio, signaling England that they had landed safely and that the area was ideally suited for further air-drops.

CHAPTER EIGHT

The next few weeks were filled with constant activity. Toward evening, on the day of the air-drop, the head of the underground communication network dropped in on the Eising farm in response to a call from Vander May. The man's name was Harmsen and he was an ordinary-looking fellow, but he was called "The Spider" because all the various underground organizations were tied together through his network of contacts. He even looked a little like a spider, with his big nose and small piercing eyes.

Mr. Harmsen was very happy to see Rudi, for his radioman had been arrested only a week earlier. He had a couple of important messages that Rudi transmitted the same night. But the next day he took Rudi with him to Assen because the radioman had to be more easily accessible than he was on the farm. Harmsen asked Vander May to see to it that the radio also arrived in Assen that day.

"And he said it as if he were asking me to deliver a loaf of bread," said Vander May laughing ruefully. "How are we going to transport that dangerous piece of hardware over the roads with Guardsmen checking everywhere?"

"Like a loaf of bread," said John. "In my delivery basket."

They fetched the baker's delivery basket from Uncle Gerrit's, and the radio fit into it with room to spare. Loaves of bread from the local bakery covered the radio completely. John put on his white jacket and pedaled to Assen with his special delivery. The trip was easy, for he had the wind behind him, and no one stopped him on the way. But when he turned into the street where he was to make his delivery, the road was blocked by Germans and Guardsmen who were conducting a spot check. He couldn't possibly risk a search here, but neither could he turn around and go back—that would certainly arouse suspicion.

But, then, he was delivering bread, wasn't he? And why shouldn't he have a customer on this street? He jumped off his bike and parked it against the fence of the nearest house, lifted the lid of his basket and took out two loaves of bread. Then he strode up to the door of the house and rang the doorbell. He leaned against the doorpost, whistling and casually looked back at the activity on the road. They were keeping an eye on him, he noticed. The door was opened by a woman carrying a small child.

"There you are, madam, two loaves."

"But . . . but . . ." she stammered.

"No, it's all right," said John. "It's bought and paid for, including ration cards. Have a nice day!"

He thrust the two loaves into her hands, tipped his cap and walked back to his bike, whistling. Now the trick was to act nonchalant. Don't look up. Turn the bike and then hop onto the seat as if everything were normal. He was pedaling away and there was no outcry from behind him. It had worked! Goodbye, you Nazi bloodhounds! Here goes your quarry. May we never meet again!

Only when he turned the corner and was safe from their eyes, did his fear catch up with him. Suddenly his legs felt tired and wobbly in the knees. So he rode slowly to Mother's place, parked the bike in the shed, and put on a cheerful expression.

"I saw you ride up," she told him. "You were carrying bread, weren't you? Are you helping out at Jansen's bakery?"

What could he say? If she knew what he was up to, she would be in terror for the rest of the war.

"What's the matter? Do you think it's beneath my dignity?" he asked, laughing.

"No, of course not! I think it's good work. As long as you don't neglect your studies. Have you seen Fritz lately?"

"Oh, sure, Mom! I see him almost every day. He's staying with a farmer in Uncle Gerrit's neighborhood, and he seems to like it pretty well. Don't worry your head about Fritz. He's getting plenty of fresh air and exercise!"

What horrible times! He couldn't even be truthful with him own mother.

When he left an hour later, the light was beginning to fade. A few blocks farther, he met Tricia on her way to see Mother. She immediately agreed to ride ahead and see whether it was safe. Everything was quiet in front of the house where the radio had to be delivered. Those inside were glad to get the bread as well as the radio.

Rudi welcomed him with a big smile. He had been standing at the attic window with The Spider when John had made his delivery earlier that day. The Spider had recognized John immediately.

"A quick-witted fellow," he had said, watching John's maneuver. "We can use more cool-headed men like that."

"So consider yourself properly decorated and knighted," said Rudi. "You staying overnight?"

John was tempted. He liked the soft-spoken young man and was eager to ask him more questions, but Tricia was waiting outside. As he was leaving, Rudi quickly pushed two chocolate bars and a pack of cigarettes into his hands. The bars he gave to Tricia who was patiently waiting around the corner; and he stopped and lit one of the cigarettes when he got out of town. It was a bit risky even there, however, for a man standing out front on his lawn suddenly sniffed the air, detecting the smell of a good prewar cigarette, and he watched with obvious interest as John rode off on his bike.

John spent the night at Uncle Gerrit's and returned to the Eising farm the following morning. When he arrived, the captain was just getting ready for his second training session. The previous day, the squad had been taught a little theory, and today the boys were going to try out their new weapons. MacBaf had planned to use a clearing in the nearby government forest for shooting practice, and Vander May was having a hard time getting it through his head that that would be asking for trouble. But the captain was a stubborn Scot. He also stubbornly refused to shave off his very English-looking little mustache, which completely contradicted his farmer's disguise.

Vander May insisted on their using the root cellar (which was now a jail for Mr. Vos) as a shooting range. The dirt would muffle the sound so that the shooting would barely be audible outside. Vos would temporarily have to be moved to the shed.

When they got to the farm where the root cellar was located, however, they discovered that it would not be necessary to move Mr. Vos. He wouldn't bother them again. In the heart of the large forest that stretched out beyond the farm lay Mr. Vos' grave.

Samuel told them what had happened. Through his daily contact with Vos, he began to like the man. Vos was always in a good mood, full of jokes, and eager to talk.

One day Samuel said to him, "I can hardly believe that you're really a traitor."

"But I'm not!" Vos assured him. "I only promised the S.D. to help them catch resistance people so that they would let me go. Wouldn't you have done the same thing? But I shouldn't have been so stupid as to tell that to your friends, because *they* immediately pegged me as a traitor."

With tears in his eyes, he swore that he was telling the truth. Even though he was being wronged, he gave his word that he wouldn't try to escape. That very night, when Samuel took him out for exercise and they wandered farther afield than usual, Vos suddenly knocked Samuel into a small canal and fled into the woods. The German shepherd was nearby chasing rabbits. When Samuel called him back, the big dog picked up Vos' trail immediately. About an hour later, they caught up with him, deep in the forest.

"And then?" asked Vander May, as Samuel stopped.

"What do you mean, 'And then?' " asked Samuel in a tremulous voice. "Your instructions were very clear when you handed me that revolver."

"You did well, Samuel. You did well," Vander May assured him, putting his hands on Samuel's shoulders. "Yes," thought John, "there had been no other choice." John reached for the hand of the man who had been forced into the role of executioner, and who now stood before them pale and trembling, and he squeezed it as a brother.

That night John couldn't sleep. Schram, Sylvia, and now Vos. Did they know what they were doing? Weren't these people all victims of conditions created by the war? In other times, perhaps they would have been decent, law-abiding citizens. He felt compelled to pray for the man's wife. She must be worried about her husband, probably looking for him every day. John closed his eyes and prayed.

The root cellar turned out to be ideally suited for their target practice. It was quite long and was lined with concrete walls. When the boys had stacked straw bales against the back wall and hung several barn lanterns from the ceiling beams, their firing range was complete. They practiced shooting with a Colt and with a Sten gun. The latter was a small machine gun that looked so unimpressive the boys first thought it was a British army reject. But it turned out to be a very effective weapon. They had only to touch the trigger to fire off a burst of bullets that set the strawbales dancing.

Among the weapons dropped from the plane was also a

larger machine gun—a Bren gun, which was fired from a tripod. There were also hand grenades, incendiary bombs, large time bombs to blow up bunkers and railway tracks, and small explosives—"pills" Vander May called them—that fit into one's pocket. Everyone on the squad was taught the use of all these weapons, and George was given several extra sessions so that, if necessary, he could serve as an instructor for other squads.

Some of the weapons were stored in the root cellar, and during the next few days the rest quickly disappeared to various corners of the country. A government car pulled up to the farm one day and loaded up a good share of the guns and ammunition for a squad in Groningen. Another day, a police boat from Friesland came chugging up the canal in front of Uncle Gerrit's house to be loaded during the night. Captain MacBaf was also picked up by the government car—to the relief of the squad, for no one wanted to risk his neck escorting that glaringly British mustache past the Nazi road patrols.

A shipment of weapons that had to go to a large town not too far from the farm was a particular headache. The plan had been to store these guns in a family vault in the town cemetery. But a branch of the S.D. had made their headquarters in the mayor's mansion, almost next door to the cemetery. From there the Germans, with the help of the local National Guard, kept a round-the-clock watch on the main road that passed in front of the house. It looked as if another place would have to be found to hide the weapons.

Vander May and John dropped in on Havinga to discuss the matter with him and to tell him that he had nothing more to fear from Vos. The blacksmith was relieved, and the cemetery vault gave him a sudden idea. From one of his friends, who owned a stable, he borrowed a funeral coach and a black horse. He also managed to get a casket and a coachman's outfit to be worn by the driver.

The next day, a small funeral procession slowly approached the checkpoint near the entrance to the cemetery. Havinga was in the driver's seat, wearing a three-cornered hat and a black cloak. Walking behind the coach, wearing neat black coats and mournful expressions, were Vander May and Steve, John and Job Eising, and Jack and Arend, each of them with a revolver in his pocket. Vander May, as the preacher, even sported a stovepipe hat.

Keeping a solemn face became quite a struggle when they saw the Germans come to attention at the side of the road, saluting respectfully. Steve quickly hid his face in a handkerchief to smother his laughter. When the procession reached the burial vault, it dissolved in hilarious laughter, temporarily unable to proceed with unloading the casket. A few members of the local resistance group were on hand to receive the weapons, but the casket was so heavy that it was still hard to handle. The gravedigger, a member of the other group, said that he had never before participated in such a jolly funeral.

That night the code words again sounded over the radio. But George was away instructing another group in the use of the weapons, and Fritz was on an errand, so Vander May asked Eising to give the word to the two divers whom he had selected to help with the air-drop.

This time the plane came on the first night that they were out. It made its first pass at two o'clock and made an even bigger drop than the previous time. Again, the official government car came by to pick up part of the shipment, and later a moving van also stopped at the farm. Steve delivered a small load by horse and wagon, the guns and ammuniton hidden under a load of beet-greens. The remainder of the air-drop was loaded onto a barge and taken away by a squad from a town in the eastern part of the province.

About this time, Vander May received a warning from The Spider to take extra precautions with future air-drops, for the Germans had learned of the weapon drops and were sending out patrols every night to try to locate the drop fields. They had plenty of men, for they had been reinforced by police troops who had fled from the south. In the northern part of the province, an entire air-drop had fallen into German hands.

Elsewhere, a cache of weapons had been discovered on a farm, and the farmer and two members of a strike squad sleeping in the haystack had been taken captive. Apparently, the Germans had managed to extort information from their captives, for soon other co-workers of the three men had been picked up. Fear and distrust were spreading like a pestilence.

Vander May decided to dissolve the squad temporarily. He sent a message to England by way of Rudi that there were to be no more air-drops for awhile. Everyone was sent home with instructions to lie low and refrain from resistance work of any kind. Until now, their area had been quiet, and Vander May wanted to keep it that way. Only the Saturday night get-togethers would continue.

But less than a week later, things came tumbling down around them. It happened so fast that they barely had time to collect their thoughts. Steve's village was hit by a major raid—a razzia, as it was called. Several truckloads of Germans and Guardsmen surrounded the village and then combed it from one end to the other, searching for divers and weapons. Although they searched every house from cellar to attic, they found little, for Uncle Gerrit had seen the trucks going by and had rushed to Reinders' house to phone the miller. The miller had quickly stopped his windmill with the damaged arm pointing skyward and had drawn attention to the alarm by blowing a horn from the top of the windmill.

Over a hundred divers were housed in the village, but only seven of then were found; however, they included the Jewish woman and child who had been brought there by Steve. Before leaving, the Germans plundered several pantries, carrying armloads of sausages and hams to their trucks. The prisoners were herded onto a hayrack and the farmer at whose place the Jews had been found was ordered to drive them to Assen. Three National Guardsmen were sent along as guards. The Germans all drove off in their trucks.

Steve had been hiding on his father's farm, and he saw the sad procession go by. He found it impossible to stay in hiding as Vander May had ordered, because he felt responsible for the woman and child. Was he supposed to let them be taken back to the camp? Not if he could help it! He tucked his Colt into his pocket, jumped on his bike, and raced after the wagon. He caught up to it along the canal. One of the guards was sitting on the wagon seat beside the driver, and the other two were walking alongside, talking and laughing.

"Hey, wait up!" Steve shouted, and the wagon came to a halt. He jumped off his bike, pulled his revolver from his pocket and shot down the nearest Guardsman. The man's companion raised his rifle, but one of the men on the wagon jumped on his back and, after a brief struggle, knocked the guard senseless with his own weapon. Meanwhile, the third Nazi had dropped his weapon and fled across the pasture.

Steve drove the wagon into the government forest and brought the woman and child to the farm where Samuel was also holed up. The man on the wagon helped his former guests find other places to hide and then went into hiding himself. The same night, however, the Germans returned to the village and seized seven farmers—one for each diver who had been freed. Among them were Steve's father and the miller who had given the warning.

John spent the night in Assen with his mother. The next day, Saturday, John rode to Uncle Gerrit's house, arriving there early in the afternoon, well before their scheduled get-together. As he came cycling up the path, he heard Uncle Gerrit's cow bellowing in the shed. The door of the house stood wide open; inside, the place was a shambles. John's heart pounded with fear. He ran over to Garth Reinders' place, where a distraught Mrs. Reinders told him that her husband and Uncle Gerrit had been picked up early that morning. She had always been kind to John, but now she blamed him for her husband's capture. She clung to his arm and tried to make him promise that he would get her husband back. He wanted to put her mind at ease, so he promised to do all that he could, but his thoughts were with Uncle Gerrit.

First, he had to do everything possible to help that dear old man. What could they charge him with? That he had called to warn the miller? The miller must have talked. Anything else? Had they found something incriminating in the house? Suddenly, he remember the revolver that he had hidden in a crack behind the pigpen. He raced back to the house. The gun was still there, but the radio, which had been hidden in the shed underneath the straw, lay smashed on the floor. That meant they also had Uncle Gerrit on possession of a radio! Just so the Germans didn't begin interrogating the others about the old man. Did Steve's father know where he went every Saturday evening?

John cycled back to Assen and through Rudi managed to get an audience with The Spider. The Spider said that he knew a friendly guard in the prison and that he would try to contact Uncle Gerrit through him. But that was all he could promise.

"How come you're so concerned about the old man?" asked The Spider. "Is he so important to your squad?"

"Uncle Gerrit?" exclaimed John. "He's our counsellor, our spiritual father. He knows everything about each of us!"

"I see. And you're afraid he's going to talk?"

"No! Of course not! If anybody can keep his mouth shut, Uncle Gerrit can."

"Then that's the most important consideration for now," said The Spider. "Yes, I'm sorry, young man, but that's the way it is. Sacrifices have to be made. But don't give up hope yet; we'll see what we can do." He looked hard at John and seemed about to add something, but then he thought better of it. With that, John was dismissed.

Dressed in his baker's outfit, he rode by the prison and scanned the tall, gloomy building just as the lights went on behind the tiny, barred window. He knew what it was like to be inside. Sacrifices . . . . "But not Uncle Gerrit, dear God, not him," he prayed with little hope. A couple children playing in the street looked up strangely at the delivery boy who rode by on his bike talking to himself.

As dusk turned to darkness, John returned to Uncle Gerrit's house. He took his revolver from its hiding place and put it in his pocket. Then he hid behind the woodshed and, with a heavy heart, waited for the others. Jack and Arend arrived together; Fritz followed right on the heels of Vander May; then came Steve. No one blamed him for what had happened. Stricken, they waited for George. But George didn't show up. What had happened to him? Was he sick, or had he too been arrested . . . or killed? If he were sick, surely he would have sent a message. Was it safe for them to stay here? But someone had to stay in case he arrived late.

"George can keep quiet. He's as tough as anybody!" said Arend.

"Sure, sure," said Vander May, sighing. "But I'll tell you guys this much: if they ever catch me, make tracks as quick as you can, because I won't promise that I'll be able to keep quiet, not even for the forty-eight hours that we agreed on. Not that I wouldn't do my utmost, mind you. But when I hear of the methods they use to get you to talk . . . ! But, who knows, maybe George wasn't picked up after all."

After a short discussion, they decided to move their headquarters to Eising's neighborhood. The Eising farm itself wasn't completely safe anymore either. But Eising would know a good place where they could lie low for awhile. John would stay behind to wait for George; he would be able to find them later through Job Eising.

When his comrades left, John fetched a Metwurst from the cellar, which the Germans had not discovered. He also found some bread and butter—he hadn't eaten since that morning. After washing his sandwich down with a glass of water, he wrapped himself in a blanket and sat down in the lee of the woodshed. In this way, he spent the night in a state midway between wakefulness and sleep. Bombers plied the darkness, first one way and then the other. One airplane was briefly silhouetted against the full moon like a black cross.

Toward morning, John heard noises by the house. Someone coughed. But it turned out to be a neighbor, coming to feed and milk Uncle Gerrit's cow. Shivering, John sneaked away and began pedaling stiffly toward Assen. The fields were white with hoarfrost, for it was a clear, quiet Sunday morning in early December. The sun came dazzling over the horizon as John reached the outskirts of town. A few minutes later, the air-raid siren began wailing, and squadron after squadron of Allied bombers appeared, glistening high in the morning sun. How could the people in Germany absorb all those bombings? He headed for Jansen's bakery, for he was afraid to let Mother see him now. She would certainly notice his grief. He dropped in on Rudi, instead; and that evening he was handed a note written in Uncle Gerrit's old-fashioned script. John's eyes flew over the words:

> Dear boys,
>
> Behave yourselves while grandpa is gone and don't play with fire because the place is highly flammable. No bellyaching now. I've got a right to go off by myself once in a while. Don't sit down on the job. There's a lot of work to do! Don't worry about me; I've got George for company. Give my heartiest greetings to Everett John in a couple months. Until we meet again—here or in our Father's house.
>
> Uncle Gerrit

John arrived at the Eising farm well after dark. By then, he had memorized the letter. The squad was staying at a neighboring farm, where the two divers who had helped with some of the air-drops were housed. When he came in through the summer kitchen, he could hear everybody talking at the same time; but when he entered the room, everyone looked at him in silence. The silence continued for some moments after John had read the letter. Just as they had feared, George had also been taken. Fritz turned his back and blew his nose. Steve reread the letter; he uttered a short laugh at Uncle Gerrit's humor, but it ended more like a sob. Vander May said nothing, but John could see the muscles in his jaws pulsing.

"See, I told you!" said one of the divers. "We might as well throw in the towel. We're sunk. You can count me out from now on."

"Fine!" said Vander May harshly. "You stay home!

We'll do quite well without you. Anyone else who feels the same way? Read Uncle Gerrit's note again. 'Don't sit down on the job,' he says."

"What's this meeting all about?" asked John.

He was quickly filled in. Last night the code words had again been broadcast. Perhaps Rudi hadn't passed their message on. So the squad had spent the night out in the field—for nothing. The plane never showed up, But a German patrol did. This morning they had found tire tracks on the dirt road close to the drop area. The drop would surely come tonight, said Vander May, and they ought to go. The weapons were still badly needed. Besides, the weather was with them: blustery, with a low cloud cover. The Germans night not even notice the airplane. It had to be risked, nevertheless.

"We'll put lookouts on both access roads," he explained. "If anything suspicious shows up, we won't use our signal lights and the plane will fly on. Otherwise, we'll collect the canisters, and in order to minimize the danger we'll bury them in the gravel pits just north of the field. Let's take along a few 'pills,' just in case. Better to blow up the whole works than to let them fall into German hands. Any objections?"

None. When the code words came over the radio again that evening, even the diver who had spoken out earlier silently began pulling on his boots. An hour later they were standing out in the middle of the field being pelted by a mixture of snow and rain. Armed with Sten guns, John ana Fritz posted themselves on the forest road leading to the village, while Jack and Arend watched the road west of the field. Vander May, Steve, Job Eising, and the two divers were to take care of the air-drop itself.

The airplane showed up before one o'clock that night. John could see the signal lights flashing over the field. The noisy machine made three passes and then disappeared. Now it was wait and see. Had German patrols spotted the airplane? If so, they ought to be here soon. In this weather, it seemed unlikely, however. Besides, the sky was full of bombers at the moment.

The two boys listened anxiously. All they heard was an occasional sound from their comrades in the field as they wrestled with the heavy canisters. Sometimes they spotted the flash from a light as the men searched the field for more supplies. The drop was going well. An hour later the coast was still clear. The gravel pits were not far away, so transporting the canisters was no big problem. Were they almost finished?

"We might as well go and give them a hand," suggested Fritz.

Just then they heard the sound of an automobile coming down the forest road. Slowly, two masked headlights approached.

"There they come!" said John. "Quick, Fritz, run and warn Josh! I'll stop them here."

"No!" said Fritz. "You go."

"Get going, Fritz! Remember, I'm second in command. That's an order!"

"Order all you want," said Fritz. "I'm not leaving you here alone!"

The lights were quickly drawing nearer. It sounded like a big engine. A van loaded with soldiers?

"How are we going to warn the others, Fritz?"

"When they hear the shooting, that will be plenty of

warning. But we'd better not wait too long! I see a light out in the field, so they're still working out there! I know what, I'll get on the other side of the road and then we'll catch them in a crossfire. You shoot first, John."

"He acts as if this all a game," thought John. His own heart was nearly jumping out of his throat! He waited until the headlights were about fifty meters away, and then he opened up with the Sten gun. He heard the bullets clattering on the hood, and one of the headlights shattered.

Higher! Aim at the windshield! Listen, that was Fritz's machine gun from the other side. Careful, little brother, don't get too close!

The vehicle slid wildly to a stop. There was loud, confused shouting, and then guns began firing back. One shot at a time. So there were no machine guns aboard. John heard the bullets crackling through the branches overhead. Regular weapons against machine guns! Come and get us! We'll have you for breakfast! There was the chatter of Fritz's Sten gun again.

Ducking into the ditch, John ran in closer, crawled up the bank on his stomach, and again opened fire. He raked the entire length of the vehicle. Incredibly, one headlight was still on. Someone uttered a strange scream, almost like a child crying.

Give them another burst. Over here, you lousy krauts, shoot over here! Fritz is just a kid! Whew! Things were really popping! A branch got clipped off right by his ear. John rolled down into the ditch and scrambled even closer to the car. Meanwhile, he heard Fritz blasting away. Hold it. Here, behind this big spruce—this was a perfect spot. From under the low-hanging branches he sprayed another

burst at the car. What was this? Were they making a run for it?

The car went roaring back down the road in reverse, its one headlight still burning. Funny that he couldn't seem to hit it. He jumped onto the road and gave them a parting round. He almost cheered. They had made the Germans turn tail and run. They had won!

The car turned at the end of the road, and gradually the sound of its engine faded in the distance.

"Fritz! Fritz, they're gone! Fritz . . . ? Where are you?"

Then it sank into his mind that he hadn't heard Fritz shooting for the last few minutes. He lunged back into the trees. "Fritz, Fritz!" he shouted, hoarse with fear.

"John . . . John!" came a faint voice out of the field. Thank goodness, he must be on his way to join the others already. Why didn't he wait, the hotshot? John ran down the road. Ahead two figures emerged from the darkness. "Who is it?" someone called out. It was Jack and Arend, who had come running across the field to give them a hand. Fritz? No, they hadn't seen Fritz. But someone had just hollered at them from the drop-site. He must be with the others.

But he wasn't with the others either. For there came Vander May and Steve cautiously skirting the woods. Job Eising and the two divers had left already. The whole air-drop had been carried safely away except for one canister, and it had to be somewhere out in the field. Jack and Arend were sent to look for it, while Vander May and Steve went with John to help him look for Fritz. With their big flashlights they soon found him. He was lying in the ditch, and the right side of his sweater was soaked with blood.

"He's been hit just below the shoulder," said Vander May, examining him. "If that's the *only* place he's been hit, he'll be okay. You two carry him into town straight to the doctor's house. I'm going to Eisings to get Captain MacBaf's parachute. I'll hang it up in a tree over there somewhere. Maybe we can make the Germans believe they were in a shoot-out with English paratroopers. We don't want a repeat of Putten."

He trotted off into the night. Steve had already gathered Fritz up into his arms and refused to surrender him. So John walked beside him, one Sten gun hanging over his shoulder and the other in his hand. Halfway to town, Fritz regained consciousness.

"John?" he said softly. "Is that you?"

"I'm right here, Fritz," said John, his voice nearly breaking with emotion.

"Good," said Fritz. "Who's carrying me?"

"Steve."

"Oh, Steve. Then I'm in . . . good hands. He's as strong as . . . as . . . ."

"Don't talk. We'll get you fixed up. Don't talk."

The doctor put a temporary bandage on the wound and told them not to worry. But he insisted that they take him to the hospital.

"I'd take him myself," said the doctor, "but I no longer have a car."

Just before daybreak, a grocer's cart pulled by a pony drew up in front of the house, and Fritz was lifted into the cart on a mattress. By that time Vander May had also arrived, along with Jack and Arend. They had brought John's and Steve's bikes. The last canister had not been found.

The doctor followed the cart to the hospital. As they turned into the street leading to the hospital, several German trucks went roaring by in the direction of the drop-field. The five remaining members of the squad reached the outskirts of the village by cutting through back yards, and from there they followed a network of trails to a couple of isolated shacks where they found temporary shelter. John's host was a broom-maker and a poacher, a rough, swarthy man full of hate for the Germans.

The next day, the man sent out his daughter, a bold, quick-witted girl of about sixteen, to see what she could discover. She came back with the news that the Germans had combed the entire village, and now long rows of soldiers were scouring the surrounding fields and forests. They had found one container and had picked up a few local men, one of whom was Job Eising. The Germans hadn't found anything in his house, but in the yard, partially ground into the mud, they had found an empty English cigarette pack.

So the squad fled again, for Job Eising knew that they had come here. In fact, he had been the one who had told them of the location some time ago. Once again, Vander May dissolved the group. The safest way, he said, was if everyone looked out for himself. They said goodbye to each other, delivered the Sten guns to the safekeeping of the poacher, who was mightily pleased by this honor, and then they scattered in all directions like hunted game.

CHAPTER NINE

But in those dark, chaotic days there was one bright spot. When John finally reached home by many back roads and detours, he was met at the door of the shed by his grinning host, Garth Reinders. He had been released that same morning because Uncle Gerrit had taken all the blame upon himself. And a good word from two prominent N.S.M. leaders in town hadn't hurt him either.

Uncle Gerrit had admitted that he had used Reinders' telephone to warn the miller, but he had convinced his interrogators that Reinders had not been in on the arrangement. Only the miller and Steve's father were still in jail. The other farmers from Steve's village had also been freed that morning, perhaps in order to make room for new prisoners. The jail was bursting at the seams with prisoners, said Reinders.

"How is Uncle Gerrit?" asked John.

Reinders shook his head pessimistically. "I haven't seen

him the last few days. But right after we were picked up, then I was, uh—what do you call it—con . . . con . . . ."

"Confronted?"

"Yeah, confronted with him a couple of times. We were hauled up in front of the brass, and they tested our stories against each other, but they didn't have any luck. Then he was fine—at least, he looked like his old self. He stood up in front of the court and talked like a lawyer, German and Dutch at the same time. He really broke them up! I remember thinking, if anybody makes it, he will. But when they turned me loose this morning, and I tried to put in a good word for him, you should have heard them!

" 'He's a kind old man,' I said. 'I think he's harmless.' 'A kind old man! Harmless!' they shouted. 'Harmless as a rattlesnake! That kind old man is a terrorist, and his house has served as a meeting place for other terrorists!' It sounded to me like they had pretty well milked your buddy George dry. I'm sorry, John, but I don't think your uncle's life is worth two cents in there.

"As far as your staying here, I don't mind. You won't find a safer place, now that I'm a proven ally of the Germans. But please, please! Stay under cover, because I don't want to end up in that place ever again. My cell was close to the interrogation room, and I'll remember those screams for the rest of my life!"

For extra security, John built a hiding place out of straw bales in the barn where he would be able to flee in case of an emergency. Then he retired to his old room. He sat there staring out across the canals for two days, and then he couldn't take it any longer. Disguised as a baker, he cycled to Assen and tried to arrange a meeting with The

Spider. With no success. The mysterious man was not to be reached. Rudi told John that he was inaccessible.

"But I've got to speak to him!" insisted John in desperation. "Something has to be done! We can't just sit still."

Rudi put a soothing hand on his shoulder and smiled a little. "Do you really think The Spider is sitting still?" he asked.

"No, but . . . ."

"Well, listen then! Vander May was here yesterday, and I hear he *did* find the chief. So don't work yourself into a lather. Take it easy!"

Take it easy. No advice was harder to follow, for his heart was with the old man who had become like a grandfather to him, and now his situation looked hopeless. "My friends must have worried about me in the same way when *I* was in prison," thought John. "And they must have prayed just as ardently as I did. But if I hadn't made that jump, what good would all those prayers have done?"

Slowly he pedaled to the village where Fritz was hospitalized. There, he found his brother looking quite alert, although he was still pale and weak. Fritz had been put into a private room—"First class!" he said—and all the nurses spoiled him and treated him like a wounded hero. The doctor told John that the bullet had been removed and that Fritz should be completely recovered in about six weeks. John wasn't sure whether to be pleased at the last bit of information. He would almost rather have been told that his brother would be out of action for the rest of the war.

He returned to his room at the Reinders farm and tried

to resign himself to the interminable hours of waiting. It was here that he saw the miracle that restored his faith and courage once again.

It was about nine o'clock in the morning, and John had one of his textbooks open in front of him, but he was absorbing little or nothing. "Freedom!" he mused. "So many sacrifices have been made in the name of freedom. It must be worth something tremendous to have so many of the best of our people die for it. And after the war, will the people really appreciate it?"

As he sat pondering, his eyes wandered outside, and in the distance he saw a solitary figure slowly approaching across the fields, following the windbreaks. It looked like an old man, bowed and stiff-legged. If he hadn't known better, he would have said it was . . . . John stood up to get a better look. And suddenly, even before his eyes confirmed it, his heart knew—it *was* Uncle Gerrit. It was impossible; it was too much to hope for, but it was true!

John leaped down the ladder, sprinted the length of the barn, almost bowling over Garth Reinders, and burst through the door, emerging right behind a huge haystack. Then he stopped, afraid to look around the haystack for fear of being disappointed. But no, there he came, lurching across the yard with his bow-legged gait. He raised the stick he was carrying in greeting and shouted, "Well, Johnny, my boy, here I am again," as if he had only been down to visit the cattle market.

John couldn't find his voice, and Garth Reinders just raised his hands and stared as if he were seeing a ghost. Uncle Gerrit stepped past them into the barn and walked toward the ladder leading to John's room. "I'd better not

go into the house," he said. "The fewer people who know I'm here, the safer we'll all be. Well, Garth, how about a cup of coffee?"

He put his walking stick, a branch that he had picked up somewhere, on John's table, and with a groan he sank into John's chair. Then he looked at them and laughed.

"You guys remind me of the story in the Bible where Peter returns from prison," he said. "You see me, but you can't believe your eyes. Right?"

"But, Uncle Gerrit, how . . . how did you get out?"

"How? The days of miracles are not yet past, my boy. As long as there's a God, there will be miracles. The whole jail is empty! All the prisoners are free!"

"Everybody? George too? And Job Eising?"

"Yes, I'll tell you the whole story. But first, how's my cow? Is someone taking care of her?"

That was the first thing on Uncle Gerrit's mind. And he needed a cup of coffee. He was parched with thirst after his long walk. Garth came up the ladder with a potful.

That morning at seven-thirty Uncle Gerrit's cell door had been opened, and in the doorway stood a slender young man—he looked a little like George—carrying a Sten gun.

"Into the hall!" he ordered. "Quickly, and without any noise. Take everything with you. You're all free!"

They moved as in a dream; they couldn't believe their eyes. But the other cells were also being opened, and the young men with Sten guns were herding the guards into one of the empty cells. It was a strike squad from the northern part of the province. They had forced their way into the prison at a time when there weren't any Germans around. Outside, two German army trucks were waiting, and thirty-one men who had been condemned to die scrambled aboard. A little later, they were riding out of the city, one truck heading for the neighboring province of Friesland, and the other dropping off those who wanted to hide close to home. Uncle Gerrit had been dropped off near the state forest, and he had walked the rest of the way.

"And George, where is he?" asked John.

"He boarded the other truck," said Uncle Gerrit. "I saw him briefly in the hall. He asked me to say goodbye for him, but he was too ashamed to look any of you in the face again. Poor boy! If you had seen him . . . ."

But John had only to look at Uncle Gerrit to see that, although he had not been beaten, perhaps because of his age, he too had suffered. He was back, however, and already chafing at the idea of sitting still. Therefore, he turned down Garth Reinders' invitation to go into hiding at his farm.

"I wouldn't be able to show my face anywhere around here," he said, "so this place would become a kind of prison too. I thought it over as I was walking over, and I decided to leave here. I've got a half-brother living near the German border who'll have something to keep me busy.

"He also has relatives in Germany on his wife's side, so he probably knows a way across the border. And I was thinking, maybe he'll take me along to visit some of his in-laws. And while we were there, who knows, maybe two innocent-looking old farmers could sniff out the whereabouts of that camp where they're holding your father. We can always scrounge something to eat along the way, and making up likely-sounding stories has never been any problem for me. I worked there for a while many years back, so I know the language—after a fashion."

Once Uncle Gerrit had decided on something, it was impossible to change his mind. About four o'clock the next morning he was ready to leave so that by daybreak he would be well out of the area where he might be recognized.

"Don't worry," he said at parting. "We'll be liberated in a few months, and I should be back before then. Otherwise, I'll send you a letter. If we can make it through the winter, we'll be okay. Keep a tight rein on Fritz when he gets out of the hospital! He'll be ready to kick up his heels."

And then John was alone in his small room once more, but now he was filled with joy and amazement at the way that God had sent help far beyond his prayers and expectations. However, again S.D. vans came roaring down the roads, stopping in front of one house after another to pick up those whose names had been dropped by the escaped prisoners. And again the jail was filled, and more local men were tortured to make them tell what they knew about the underground.

Weapon caches were found here and there. The air-drop hidden in the gravel pits was also discovered. Now and again a house was raided in the middle of the night and the owner shot down on his own doorstep. Anyone who had the slightest contact with the underground avoided sleeping at home nights.

In this rule of terror there was one comfort: it couldn't last much longer. The Germans had launched a powerful counter-attack in the Ardennes, but two weeks later their offensive had been completely broken up by the

Americans, and now the Germans were being driven back. The Allies were finally starting to penetrate the German border. But in Limburg, the front was still at the Meuse River, and strong German defenses awaited the Allies at Venlo and Roermond. In the middle of the winter, the Germans chased all the inhabitants out of both cities, forcing thousands of people to seek shelter and food in the agricultural areas of eastern Holland.

These refugees were joined by the starving masses from the large cities in the west. For the Germans had carried out their threat to stop food shipments to the urban areas if the railway strikers didn't return. Rations had been cut so severely in the cities that no one could survive on that allowance alone. An adult ration for one day was two small potatoes, two thin slices of bread, a paper-thin slice of cheese, and a piece of meat the size of a sugar cube. Those who didn't want to starve had to deal on the black market.

But food prices there had climbed completely out of sight for most people. A bushel of potatoes cost about 250 guilders, a bushel of wheat about 750 guilders, and a loaf of bread 65 guilders. Eventually, money became almost worthless, and food became unavailable at any price. So people began going directly to the farmers for food.

This was the task of women and children and old men, for any able-bodied man caught on the road was in danger of being picked up and sent to Germany. Even in rain or snow a sallow stream of hungry people took to the road out of the city on worn-out shoes and on bicycles without tires, with baby buggies, pushcarts, and knapsacks. Some had their last money in their pockets, but they discovered that it would buy almost nothing. People were reverting to the barter system. A sheet would bring a small bagful of potatoes or a few pounds of peas. A watch or a gold pin, shoes or a winter coat could be traded for a little meat or bacon, or maybe for eggs or flour.

Thousands and thousands of starving people braved the winter weather to trek from one farm to another, begging for food, holes in their shoes, without stockings, and often coatless. They wandered on and on, foraging farther and farther from home, and spending the nights in some farmer's barn, often with dozens of other people. They clutched their few goods in their hands or tied them about their waists, afraid someone else might steal them.

Some farmers gave until they had nothing left themselves. But there were others who saw a chance to get rich quickly, turning away anyone who didn't offer them silver or gold. But most of the pilgrims eventually received something to take home, and then they had to make the long, hazardous trip back. They might be stopped by Germans or National Guardsmen who confiscated whatever food they had spent so much energy to obtain. Sometimes their battered old bikes gave out and sometimes, too, the people themselves collapsed with exhaustion.

The ones who reached Drenthe, John's home province, were only the most tenacious and the strongest, for the trip from the urban West took several days on foot. Those that did make it were usually at the end of their strength. Once John saw two teen-age boys from Amsterdam pushing the body of their father back home on a pushcart. He lay beside the small food supply that had killed him. Starved for so long, his body had been unable to absorb a regular meal of beans and bacon.

On another occasion, as he was returning home from the hospital, John found a woman lying unconscious at the side of the road beside an old bike. He sent for Garth Reinders, who came to pick her up with a horse and wagon. At the Reinders' farm, she soon began to recover.

She told of unbearable misery and suffering in the big cities. She was from The Hague, where her husband and three small children waited for her return. Her husband was a bookkeeper, but there was no work for him. All offices, stores, and schools were closed. The people thought of nothing except getting something to eat. Most were surviving on tulip bulbs and sugar beets, made palatable by starvation. These were cooked on small stoves adapted to operate on a minimum of fuel, for coal and firewood were almost impossible to get. In the parks and along the streets, most trees had long since been chopped down. Now when people discovered that a house or apartment was vacant, they broke in and tore up the floors and walls for firewood.

Such great numbers of people were dying from starvation and cold that there were not enough coffins and hearses to give them all burial. Bodies were carried to the cemetery on ladders and pushcarts. Sometimes the death was kept a secret, and the corpse was buried in the back yard or in the cellar so that the survivors could continue to collect their ration cards.

Added to all this misery in The Hague was the fear of the V-1 rockets that the Germans were launching at England; for every so often one of them would fizzle and drop short, wiping out half a block of homes. Once, a horse was hit by a bomb fragment, and the people in the surrounding houses, seeing the animal go down, threw themselves upon it with knives and axes. Within half an hour, all that remained was a bloody spot on the pavement.

The woman from the city left again for following morning on another bicycle loaded with food supplies. But her stories of starvation circulated in the area, and the country people began to forget their own troubles and dangers in their eagerness to help their fellow sufferers in the cities. Moreover, with so many strange people on the road, it was becoming less dangerous to move around.

Once again Vander May called the squad together, this time to organize efforts to gather food and to try to transport them to the starving West. A few daring boatmen were willing to take supplies across Lake Yssel to Amsterdam. The churches pooled their efforts and sent many truckloads of supplies to suffering areas, sometimes complete with papers stamped by a sympathetic German commandant.

One day Rita drove up to the Reinders' farm in a car equipped with a gas converter. An old mechanic had agreed to drive her and another nurse to Rotterdam to deliver food. Garth Reinders slaughtered one of his largest pigs, and several other farmers also contributed foodstuffs so that the car was completely loaded in two days. By bribing the German guard on the Yssel Bridge with a ham and a bottle of gin, Rita and her companions managed to deliver their load.

The flood of starving wanderers continued until the end of February. All the farmers in the area did their best to help, with one exception. One rich farmer aroused the indignation of all the local people by charging one guilder apiece for his eggs and twenty guilders for a pound of butter.

"He has to be taught a lesson," pronounced Vander May. This was the first time that Fritz was back with the group. He had been discharged from the hospital just a few days earlier, and he had joined John in the room over the Reinders' barn. That way, John could keep an eye on him.

The following night, the six of them cycled to the big farm and rousted the farmer out of bed. With drawn revolvers, they forced the farmer and his wife and their two servants into the living room. Then they searched the closets and cellar for supplies. Their efforts produced a large stockpile of beef, bacon, vegetable oil, wheat, and several jars of lard.

"This is your donation to your starving countrymen, right?" said Vander May.

"Y-y-yes, sir," said the farmer, terrified.

But his wife was less easily intimidated. "You resistance people have to pay like anybody else," she said. "What will you give us for all that?"

"Nothing," said Vander May.

"Then you people are no better than thieves!" she shouted.

"No," replied Vander May calmly. "It's *you* who are the thieves, charging outrageous prices to starving people! Ours is nothing but an act of justice. You've made your share of profit already. We should also take your money box."

"Oh, please, sir!" begged the farmer, nearly beside himself.

"Pipe down!" snapped Vander May, with contempt. "We're not going to touch your precious money! Just get us something to drink, if you please. You've given me a dry throat."

The maid fetched a large pitcher of milk and poured a glass for each of them.

"What do we owe you for the milk?" Vander May asked after draining his glass.

The farmer and his wife put their heads together for a whispered consultation.

"Twenty cents," he answered.

"Now that's a fair price," said Vander May. "You're beginning to learn. Here's a quarter. Keep the change."

"Thank you," said the farmer, looking relieved. The male servant suddenly snorted in laughter; then he hurried to help the men load the supplies on their bikes.

"He's not a bad fellow really," he confided outside. "But his wife is terribly greedy! How do I let you know if they go on charging black market prices?"

"Just tie a piece of twine around the fencepost by the gate. Then we'll come back for another visit," said Vander May.

But as winter began to yield to spring, the fencepost remained bare, and then suddenly the stream of hungry wanderers stopped. The German soldiers guarding the Yssel Bridge had received orders to turn everyone back. They were told that the roads had to be kept clear for military traffic. The day of liberation appeared to be drawing closer, for the Americans had finally crossed the Rhine. Somewhere in Germany, near Remagen, they had captured a bridge intact, and from there they were fanning out in all directions, also toward the Dutch border.

In their hearts, most German soldiers knew that war was lost. But they had been ordered to fight to the end, and in their desperation, many became even more vicious. When

General Rauter, the top German officer in the country, was ambushed and seriously wounded on a lonely road going across the Gelderland heaths, more than one-hundred captured resistance people were taken to the scene and shot. In other towns, too, men were taken out of prison and executed.

One day Vander May told the squad that Rudi, the young radio man from England, had also been killed. The Germans had discovered his location with special radio-tracking equipment and had surrounded the house. Rudi had chosen to fight to the death rather than fall into German hands. The news rankled in John's heart. Why did the cheerful, soft-spoken young man have to get killed so near the end of the war?

By this time liberation was imminent, for Canadian and American troops were advancing rapidly across the eastern tip of Gelderland and Overyssel. Many Dutch Nazis were again fleeing to Germany. Vander May decided to enlarge the squad by inviting the poacher and the divers who had helped at the last air-drop to join. Now they had eleven men. Every man was given blue overalls and an orange armband.

Jack and John were sent out to make sketches of all the German defenses in the area, and Steve and Fritz made visits to people in Assen and Groningen to get information about German troop concentrations. A few days after they returned, the fighting was so close that they could hear the rumble of artillery fire.

Then Vander May prepared to leave, for he wanted to slip through the German lines in order to bring the information that they had collected to the Allies. He split the squad into three teams, each with a different task. John and Fritz were given the job of blowing up an earthen bunker that had been built along the canal by the Germans about one hour away from Uncle Gerrit's house. They had to pick up the explosives for the job at the farm where Samuel was staying.

They headed for the place at dusk, dressed like farmers. Everywhere they went people were standing outside in eager anticipation. At one point they met a group of National Guardsmen speeding north on their bikes with their rifles slung across their backs. A man emerged from a house and joined them. One of the neighbors standing outside watching said that the men were headed for the big dike across the top of Lake Yssel which led to the western part of the country.

As they turned right at an intersection, John and Fritz suddenly found themselves in the midst of a platoon of retreating German soldiers. They were sprawled in the ditch on both sides of the road, and their bikes were parked against the trees. They looked tired and disheveled, but they seemed to be in a good mood. They were passing around a big bottle. One of them tottered up to the two boys and asked them how to get to Assen.

"Just go straight ahead," said John. "But if you turn right, that road will take you straight to Germany."

"Yah!" shouted one of the men in German. "Back home to Germany! We're going home to Mom!" They laughed and waved as the boys rode on.

"Heil Hitler!" shouted Fritz, waving back. "That looks hopeful," he said to John. "It looks like they've stopped fighting."

"Yes, but they're regular army," said John. "The gung-ho party men, the S.S., may feel a whole lot different!"

When they got to the farm, there, too, the whole family was standing outside under the darkening sky. The Jewish woman was still at the farm too, and her daughter came dashing out to meet them, asking whether they had more chocolate. The farmer told them that Canadian troops were only a few kilometers away. He had cycled southward earlier that day and had seen the first Allied tanks.

"Then why aren't they here yet?" asked Sam nervously. "Just wait and see, tomorrow the Germans will be back again." There was more fear than hope in his eyes.

But everyone else was optimistic enough to laugh at his gloomy prediction. Early the next morning, as John and Fritz were leaving with a heavy satchel of explosives on the back of John's bike, the artillery fire sounded closer than ever. As they neared the bunker, the sun was just beginning to show on the horizon. The bunker was a huge earthen structure reinforced by big wooden poles sunk into the ground and with machine gun emplacements facing south. There wasn't anyone to be seen in the area.

"I wonder if it serves any purpose to blow this thing up," mused John aloud. "It doesn't look like the Germans plan to use it."

"Maybe not, but it should be fun," said Fritz. "Come on, let me set the dynamite!"

"Nothing doing! I'll handle that. You just stand on lookout."

The dark cavern smelled musty inside. Placing the charges was a tense job. John's fingers trembled. He had a twenty-minute timer, but suppose it was faulty . . . .

But the connections were made, and John raced outside with a gasp of relief. He wanted to hop on his bike and leave, but Fritz persuaded him to stay and watch their handiwork. A narrow path passed the bunker and led across a field. They followed it several hundred meters to a row of bushes that would afford them some cover.

"There's someone watching us from that farmhouse over there," said Fritz.

"Let him watch," said John. "Fifteen minutes to go."

They dropped down on their stomachs behind the bushes and peered out between the branches. The sun was well above the horizon now, and a skylark burst forth in a song of jubilation. It promised to be a beautiful spring day.

"Eight minutes to go!"

An old farmer came pedaling his bike along the canal.

"Look, John! Shall I warn him?"

"Let him go. There's plenty of time for him to get clear."

Six minutes . . . five minutes . . . . The old man was almost up to the bunker now. Hurry up, old fellow! To their consternation, the old man stopped, then dismounted and laid down his bike. He was going to look inside. He must have been curious about what the boys had been doing there with their satchel.

John and Fritz jumped up, shouting and waving. John fired into the air and motioned frantically to the old man.

"Get out of there! Quick! Hurry!"

The man had stopped at the entrance, staring at them in surprise. But when the boys came running toward him and John shot into the air again, he slowly trudged back to his bike, picked it up, put one foot on the pedal, pushing off a couple of times with the other. Then he swung his leg over the seat and was finally on his way. He was about one hundred meters down the path when the bunker exploded, sending dirt flying high into the air. The two boys dropped to the ground, and when they looked up, through a cloud of dust they could see the farmer scooting across the field like a frightened rabbit. They laughed until their sides ached.

They returned to the Reinders farm by following back roads. Flying over the canal at a height of several hundred meters, came a small plane, zig-zagging back and forth. A reconnaissance plane. It turned northward and began circling a meadow. A few gunshots rang out. Then came the whine of a shell, and a geyser of smoke and flame rose from the meadow. Mrs. Reinders ran for the house. The war was right on their doorstep.

"A platoon of German soldiers dug in on that meadow this morning," said Garth. "That plane must have them spotted."

"Then the Canadians must be real close!" cried Fritz. "I bet we could see them from the upstairs window."

He lunged up the ladder with John right on his heels. But all they could see from the window was a burning farmhouse. Black smoke spread out over the countryside. The small window reverberated with the pounding of the artillery.

"They'll be here any minute!" Fritz said excitedly. "Come on, John, let's get our armbands on. Oh, man-oh-man, isn't this something!"

"We'll put them in our pockets," said John. "Where's your Sten gun?"

Suddenly they heard voices downstairs—German voices. John and Fritz crept to the edge of the hatch. Beneath them stood four German soldiers—three older men and one young fellow in a uniform much too large for him. They were asking Reinders for something to eat and drink. They had eaten nothing for two days, they said.

"I refuse food to no one who needs it," said Garth. "My wife will fix you some sandwiches. Meanwhile, take a load off your feet and relax. Fighting is useless anyway. You've got to know that the war is lost."

The three older soldiers nodded wearily, but the youngest one got very angry.

"Lost?" he cried. "Nothing is lost! We'll be back! We'll win yet. Our Fuehrer says . . . ."

"Okay, okay," said Garth soothingly, "but now just rest for a while. Here's my wife with milk and sandwiches."

The Germans put their rifles against the wall and sat down on a pile of sacks to eat. Garth stood beside them. John and Fritz looked at each other. Each understood what the other was thinking without saying a word. John slipped the orange armband over his sleeve. Fritz did the same. Then they quietly descended the ladder and suddenly appeared before the sitting men with their Sten guns.

"Hands up!" John ordered in German.

Three of the soldiers raised their hands immediately, completely surprised, but the young fellow leaped up and dove for the rifles. Garth tripped him up, however, and shoved him back among the others, who grabbed him and held him down. He was sobbing wildly.

"Don't blame him," said one of the older soldiers. "He doesn't know any better. He was raised with the Hitler youth."

The soldiers were searched and their gunbelts confiscated; then they were allowed to finish their sandwiches. Suddenly Mrs. Reinders came rushing into the barn. From outside came the sound of confused shouting and cheering.

"One of those big noisy things is coming across the bridge!" she said. "And people are hanging out their flags!"

Fritz ran outside and came prancing back in.

"They're here!" he shouted jubilantly. "I saw the tanks! Shall we go?" They told their prisoners to put the remaining bread into their pockets and marched them outside in single file.

"Forward march!" said John.

People converged on the main road from all sides. Tanks with huge, imposing guns went clattering by. Out of the hatches, dirty but smiling faces received the enthusiastic welcome of the people. A little girl approached one of the tanks with an armload of flowers. The tank stopped and the little girl climbed up the tread, gave her flowers to one of the men, and got a kiss in return. The people cheered and laughed, and the streets were bright with the red, white, and blue colors of the long-forbidden flag fluttering from almost every window. Riding with a Canadian officer in a jeep came Vander May. He jumped out and strongly embraced John and Fritz and also a woman standing nearby who was weeping with joy.

Then someone began singing the national anthem.

CHAPTER TEN

The Canadians arrived on a Thursday in mid-April, and it was several days before the exuberance of liberation diminished somewhat.

The following Sunday the churches were crowded. Now John could sit beside Mother and his younger brothers and sisters—and next to Rita, who had come from Friesland. As the congregation joined in singing a Psalm of praise to God, he realized how much he had missed this during all the months that he had been in hiding.

He felt Mother's hand reaching for his, and as she squeezed his hand, he understood what was going through her mind: "It's over, and at least I still have you and Fritz and all the other children." He glanced at her out of the corner of his eye. She wasn't singing, and tears were running down her cheeks. He also understood the tears. He could hear Father saying, "One of us must survive, John!" If only Father, too, were returned to them, safe and sound. How long would they have to wait to find out?

The next day John was back at his job as second-in-command in the area where he had been hiding. That morning he had attended a meeting at the town hall where Vander May had set up his office as the local commandant. Now it was early afternoon, and he was cycling back home, wearing his blue overalls and orange armband. The weather was bright and clear, and the farmers were out in the fields getting ready for planting. Busy plowing, they gave John a friendly wave as he rode by.

It was wonderful to be free again, to live without fear and to be able to go wherever you wished without danger of being picked up. John could not seem to get used to the feeling. Each day anew he found it hard to believe. It was like a miracle! Last night when he was in bed, a car had suddenly stopped in front of the house, and he had leaped out of bed in sudden fear. Germans? But then he remembered. No, that was over for good.

From the canal came a muffled explosion. A group of boys were playing with hand grenades that they had found somewhere. They tossed one into the canal and cheered as a geyser of muddy water shot up into the sky and a few dead fish floated to the surface. But they scattered across the fields when they saw him coming. He recognized two of them and took down their names for the local police. All ammunition that was found had to be turned in. In a neighboring town, two boys had been seriously wounded when they tried to dismantle a grenade that they had found.

At a farm close to the bridge, a large squad of Canadian soldiers had set up camp in the farmyard. One of them was preparing his dinner. He emptied a couple of cans into a little pan, then he scooped a shallow hole in the ground, emptied a half can of gas into the hole and tossed his cigarette into it. He held his little pan over the leaping flames until they died out. A group of soldiers lay sprawled on a piece of canvas playing cards, and two small children circled them begging for gum.

On the road in front of the house a big truck crammed with German prisoners braked to a stop. The truck had to wait for a long column of vehicles and tanks crossing the bridge from the other side. The Canadian soldiers sauntered over to the truck and began needling the Germans.

"Hi there, you krauts. Stinking Jerries! Hitler kaput!"

But the prisoners looked straight ahead and didn't respond. One Canadian, a big, tough-looking fellow, climbed up onto the truck and stripped watches and rings off several of the Germans. But the truck started moving, and as he jumped off the back, he took a nasty spill. A loud cheer and laughter went up from the other Canadian soldiers, and one of them ran after the truck and tossed a pack of cigarettes to the prisoners.

Across the road, at the edge of a plowed field stood four simple wooden crosses. They marked the graves of four Canadian soldiers. The roads of the Allied advance were lined with such crosses. And German soldiers, too, lay buried along the roadsides.

"People are still dying," thought John. "When will it be completely over? Will the German beast ever surrender? Or will he have to be killed in his lair, as Churchill said?"

A jeep went speeding past him carrying two soldiers. Then it suddenly slammed to a halt, skidding onto the shoulder, as one soldier looked back at John. He jumped out of the jeep and ran toward John with open arms. He was a skinny redhead.

"You ugly old sun-of-a-gun!" he shouted. "First you let me think for over a year that you've been killed, and then you make yourself so hard to find nobody knows where you are. Even Uncle Gerrit . . . ."

"William! Is that you, you foul-mouthed redhead!"

"How are you, brother? Good old John!"

They clasped hands in a long handshake and looked each other over, poking and touching as if they couldn't believe their eyes. John found it amazing that this gum-chewing Canadian soldier was the same fellow his family had sheltered early in the war and who had become his closest friend.

"All anybody knew was that you had moved in with your mother," said William. "I spent all day yesterday driving around Assen."

"What did you say about Uncle Gerrit?"

"Oh, he didn't know where . . . ."

"So he's back?"

"Sure! He's been back since Saturday. He knows where to find your father. And he told me about your plan to pick him up. I'm all for it, and I'm coming along! I can line up a car."

"No need! We've already got one—a German army truck. Right now, other guys are using it to round up N.S.M. members who didn't run for Germany."

"I'll see we get something better—a regular car. I can also get us the necessary papers. What are we doing, standing here! Get rid of your bike and jump in."

"I can't, William. I've got a job to do here!"

"What do you do?"

"I'm second-in-command in the local branch of the Inland Battle Forces."

"Well, then appoint a third-in-command and let *him* do your work. I'm not letting you slip out of my hands now! Come on, what makes you think you're irreplaceable?"

John parked his bike at a nearby farmhouse and came running back to the jeep. William introduced John to his companion, "This is Nick, my chauffeur."

"Hi!" said Nick, chewing on a great wad of gum. He took off so fast that John almost fell out of the jeep. First they went to the house where John had been given an office, and he turned his command over to Steve and told him that he wouldn't be back for a while. Then they drove to Uncle Gerrit's place. On the way there, William told John what he had been doing over the past year.

After Uncle Henry had been killed, he and Leo had joined another group. During the winter he had been sent to the liberated south with a message. He had crossed the German lines through the swamps around Dordrecht, pulling a small boat through the tall reeds. And now he was serving as a liaison officer and interpreter.

"It's a good job," said William. "I'll get them to measure you for a uniform too. That will make it easier for us to travel in Germany."

"And Leo?" asked John. "What about Leo?"

"I don't know," said William. "But I did see Angie. She made it. Hold up, Nick! Take this small road to the left."

They backed up, and in a big cloud of dust they followed the little dirt road leading to Uncle Gerrit's house. As they approached, John could see the old man outside, spading his garden. When he saw John, his face lit up and he shouted, "Tomorrow I'm going to plant spinach at the old place, John! And just wait and see, your father will be the one to harvest it!"

Uncle Gerrit invited them all in for coffee, but Nick refused. He couldn't follow their conversation anyway, he said. He picked up Uncle Gerrit's shovel and began digging where the old man had stopped. Uncle Gerrit told them that he and his brother had succeeded in tramping far into Germany. No, they had experienced no trouble whatsoever, for children and old people were completely ignored. They had located the camp and had marked it on a map.

Uncle Gerrit had even talked to prisoners who were working outside the camp, and they had assured him that there was a De Boer in the camp, and that he was doing all right. He wore a red triangle on his prison uniform, they said, which meant that he was a political prisoner. So that part fit. Most of the men in that particular camp wore green triangles, which meant that they were common criminals—thieves and murderers. Uncle Gerrit had told the men to pass on his greetings to De Boer and had given them a ham sandwich to forward to him. Uncle Gerrit was curious about whether he had gotten the sandwich.

"Ask him yourself," said William. "You're coming along to pick him up."

"No thanks," said Uncle Gerrit. "You know who you should take along? Rita, or some other nurse. From what I saw and heard . . . , but no, I won't say anymore. You may need her, though."

When they went outside, Nick was still digging. He looked up at Uncle Gerrit for approval.

"Good night!" mumbled Uncle Gerrit in Dutch. "It looks like somebody dropped a bomb in my yard! Some gardener!" But he patted Nick on the shoulder and said in broken English, "Goot! You be a goot digger. Who do I supposed to bury in dat hole? Hitler? De sooner de better!"

Nick laughed and spat his gum far out into the garden.

"I think," Uncle Gerrit said seriously to the two boys, "that never before have so many people prayed for the death of a man as they do for Hitler's. I pray for his death every day. While that madman is sitting safe in his bunker in Berlin, thousands of people are dying for him every day that he keeps this war going!"

William kept John with him the rest of the day. They dropped in on Mother and Rita. And then William introduced John to his commanding officer. He also showed John the car that he had picked out for their trip to Germany, a big Dodge which had been confiscated from a N.S.M. man.

Then it was a matter of wait and see whether Uncle Gerrit's prayers would be answered. Meanwhile, John kept busy at the job before him: questioning N.S.M. members, collecting ammunition, getting Garth Reinders—who had been arrested as an N.S.M. member—back out of prison. He had to discipline the poacher for abusing prisoners and for shaving off the hair of an N.S.M. girl. A list had to be made of all the German graves in the area in order to have the bodies transferred later. All the goods confiscated from N.S.M. members had to be stored somewhere and trustworthy people found to oversee the place. And Fritz had to be talked to. He refused to go back to school and, like William, he wanted to go fight the Japanese in Indonesia.

Meanwhile, Germany was fighting its last battle. All of the Netherlands had now been liberated except the western provinces of North and South Holland, where widespread starvation was threatening. The Swedish Red Cross sent flour that was used to bake bread, but it didn't go very far among five million hungry people.

Then things began to move fast, however. Mussolini came to a bloody end in Italy. The Americans and the Russians met at the Elbe. English bombers got permission from the German authorities to drop food supplies on airfields in the still-occupied provinces and they dropped thousands of food parcels. This happened on the last Sunday in April. The following day came the news of Hitler's death. He had committed suicide in his Berlin hideout. At last, the world was free of that servant of satan.

John got a note from William. It was very short: "Be ready to leave!"

But if took five more days before General Montgomery, in his headquarters on the heaths of Lueneburg, accepted the unconditional surrender of the German army. The following day, the German forces holding western Holland also surrendered. The order to surrender was signed in Wageningen in the presence of Prince Bernhard. Hundreds of trucks loaded with food were standing ready and, as soon as the surrender was official, they sped into the starving provinces. It was the fifth of May, a day of thanksgiving and celebration. Finally, the whole country was freed from the yoke of slavery under which it had suffered for five years.

Early the next morning a big black Dodge, with Nick behind the wheel, pulled up in front of the house. They set out immediately, and the trip went without any hitches. They hardly noticed the border crossing. Now and then they were stopped by Polish or American soldiers, but one look at the papers William had secured from his commanding officer was always sufficient. Whenever they needed gas, they drove into an American camp and got all that they wanted. Once, when they got thirsty, they drove onto the yard of a German farm, and the farmer bowed and smiled and told them that they were welcome to whatever they wished. William settled for a few bottles of beer, and Rita came back to the car with two jars of canned cherries.

"They're for your father," she told John. "They'll be easy on his stomach."

The Dodge ran well, and Uncle Gerrit's map was excellent. But every so often they had to detour for a bombed-out bridge, that is, if the Americans hadn't rigged up a temporary one. And the roads had been ruined in many places by tanks, so that even Nick couldn't make very good time. On one occasion, when they were passing through a town that had been completely reduced to rubble, they got lost among the ruins.

Night had fallen before they approached the camp. They no longer talked. Their throats ached with suspense. All John's thoughts were reduced to a prayer that he repeated over and over: "Lord, let him be alive!"

A large sign flashed by: *Konsentrationslager* (Concentration Camp). Small groups of men in striped suits were walking casually along the road, smoking. From behind a high barbed-wire fence, more prisoners eyed them curiously. Rows of barracks. A large gate. American guards.

John left everything in William's hands. They drove into the camp, got out and were immediately surrounded by prisoners, all talking at the same time. A few Dutchmen were among them. All had bald heads, dark, hollow eyes, and a foul, overpowering smell—the horrible smell of Westerbork.

"De Boer . . . ? De Boer, oh, he's dead."

"What did you say?"

"De Boer died several months ago. Typhoid, I think."

"Ah, you're nuts! That was somebody else."

"Sure, that was Boer. Peter Boer. Who are you looking for? Peter who?"

"Everett John. Everett John De Boer. His son is here for him."

"Oh, you mean *him*. Why didn't you say so?"

"Get Everett John!"

"That's the fellow that got all his teeth kicked out. Sure he's here. Everybody knows him."

"So he's alive? He's not *dead*?"

"No, of course not. They couldn't kill old Everett. Hey, Everett John!"

"Hey, Everett John!" several men shouted. "Your son's here!"

They were all looking at the same barracks. The door was standing open. A man appeared in the doorway wearing a striped suit like all the others. He was walking with a cane, slightly stooped.

"That's not him," John was about to say. But then he looked again. Yes, it was Father, but he looked like Grandfather, who had died a few years before the start of the war.

"Don't act shocked," William said in his ear. "Don't blubber. You'll only upset him."

They embraced each other wordlessly. The onlookers stood by, suddenly quiet.

A half hour later, they were on the return trip. Father and one of his friends, who was in much poorer shape, were in the back seat tended by Rita. John and William sat in the front with Nick. It was hard to drive off and leave all those other men behind, for all of them had but one thought—to get home. William promised that he would be back. He gave them his word. As soon as possible, he would return with a truck. But all those hollow, longing eyes followed them until they were out of sight.

John was almost sitting backwards in his seat.

"That's my Dad!" he said. "That's my Johnny!" said Father laughing. "You guys are quite something—coming to get their father out of the camp themselves!"

"Thank you," said William. "That's the nicest thing I've heard in a long time."

"What do you mean?"

" '*Their* father,' you said. So you called me your son."

"But, of course! And that goes for you too, Rita."

"Thank you . . . , Dad." It was the first time that she had called him that.

"I hope your parents will also be free soon, William."

"I'm going over there to help free them," said William. "And Fritz wants to come too."

"It has to be done," said Father. "I'm afraid I wouldn't be much help, the shape I'm in now." He grinned. "How do you like my smile?"

"No matter, Dad. With a set of false teeth, you'll be as good as new in no time! The important thing is that you're back with us again. We're all back together!"

"Thank God!" said Father.

And a little while later, he repeated softly, "Thank God!"

Father's friend moaned. His emaciated body could hardly stand the jouncing of the car. They stopped at a farm and asked the farmer for pillows. When the man hesitated, they let him look in the back seat. Then he gave up his pillows without a murmur.

Nick carefully picked his way along the rubble-strewn roads and between the bomb craters. A long, difficult journey lay ahead of them.

A journey through the night.

But the journey through the night of war and anxiety and terror was over! It was a miracle, they all felt, that they had been spared to see the coming of the new day.